IN THE
FATHER'S
HANDS

IN THE
FATHER'S
HANDS

MAKING CHRIST THE
LORD OF YOUR LIFE

J. OSWALD
SANDERS

Discovery House®
from Our Daily Bread Ministries

In the Father's Hands:
Making Christ the Lord of Your Life

Discovery House is affiliated with
Our Daily Bread Ministries, Grand Rapids, Michigan.

Requests for permission to quote from this book should be directed to:
Permissions Department, Discovery House,
PO Box 3566, Grand Rapids, MI 49501,
or contact us by email at permissionsdept@dhp.org.

Interior design by Rob Williams, InsideOutCreativeArts.com

Library of Congress Cataloging-in-Publication Data

Names: Sanders, J. Oswald (John Oswald), 1902–1992, author.
Title: In the Father's hands : making Christ the Lord of your life / J. Oswald Sanders.
Description: Grand Rapids : Discovery House, 2019. | Summary: "Connect with the Creator of the universe and use the power of the Holy Spirit to live as disciples of Christ, These ninety daily readings centered on Scripture will help you grow to become the Christ-follower you desire to be"—Provided by publisher.
Identifiers: LCCN 2019030863 | ISBN 9781627079556 (paperback)
Subjects: LCSH: Bible—Meditations. | Christian life—Meditations.
Classification: LCC BS491.5 .S28 2019 | DDC 242/.2—dc23
LC record available at https://lccn.loc.gov/2019030863

Printed in the United States of America
First printing in 2019

CONTENTS

Contents

PART 2
LORD OF THE EVERYDAY

PART 3

LORD OF OUR FUTURE

Contents

Introduction

J. Oswald Sanders was an international Christian preacher, missionary statesman, prolific author, and gifted administrator who went to be with the Lord on October 24, 1992. He is primarily remembered for his Christian classic *Spiritual Leadership*, which continues to be widely distributed. That book still has a major impact on Christian leaders, both prominent and little known, around the world. Charles Colson (1931–2012), the founder of Prison Fellowship, for example, called it the best volume on spiritual leadership ever written.

The central theme of Oswald's works is discipleship, which is as important in our age of social media and internet connectivity as it was when Oswald wrote these words in the mid-to-late 1900s. Believers still struggle to maintain faithful and vibrant fellowship with Jesus Christ. As committed as we might be to staying close to God in our day-to-day lives, a changing society and our myriad responsibilities tend to tear us away from Him. Oswald's deep, thoughtful challenges can help us to stay anchored in our faith and to remain safely nestled in the Father's hands.

These devotional thoughts—excerpted from seventeen of Sanders's books—remind us of what our Lord has done for us in the past, provide guidance for staying close to Him in our everyday lives, and excite us about our future connection to our Savior for all eternity. There's not a portion of our lives that is not addressed in these ninety Scripture-based and life-challenging readings.

From the pen of one of Christianity's finest leaders of the twentieth century comes timeless truths for us as we charge forward for Jesus in the twenty-first century. May J. Oswald Sanders's insights and words of encouragement help you grow in your Christian life and experience the peace that comes from being in the Father's hands.

—The Publisher, 2019

PART 1

LORD
OF OUR
PAST

Necessity for Preparation

Isaiah 40:2

I n dramatic yet tender language, the prophet Isaiah brought God's message to His chastened people. "'Comfort, O comfort My people,' says your God. 'Speak kindly to Jerusalem'" (Isaiah 40:1–2 NASB). That wooing note of love must have evoked a warm response in the heart of exiles pining for their homeland.

An assurance of pardon (40:2). First, he told them that though the nation's sin had been extreme, it had been pardoned; and her warfare, or hard service, had ended. The divine discipline had achieved its purpose, and the penalty of her iniquity had been accepted as paid off. Now the grace of God could be freely expressed toward her.

The necessity for preparation (40:3–4). Next the prophet stressed what they must do if the glory of God were again to be revealed in their midst. "Make smooth in the desert a highway for our God" (v. 3 NASB). In the East, a victorious general, returning from his conquest, was given the victor's triumphal march. History records titanic feats of engineering in making perfect roads through the trackless desert for the conquering hero. Every low place was filled, every high place reduced, every uneven place leveled, so that the conqueror might enjoy unimpeded progress.

John the Baptist referred to that custom when describing his function as forerunner of the Messiah (Matthew 3:3). But it also enshrines an important and contemporary spiritual principle. If God is to reveal himself in special blessing to His people, there must be spiritual preparation. John's task was to create in the nation such a sense of sin and repentance as would make it possible for the Holy Spirit to work in power among them.

It must be this way among God's people today. Anything in this life must be straightened, any stumbling blocks removed. Low levels of spiritual living must be raised and rough elements of character polished. Areas of neglect must be remedied and relationships adjusted. This is something for which we alone are responsible, but the Holy Spirit will empower us to do it. (EI)

A Purpose for Each Life

Psalm 32:8–9

I believe God has an individual will for my life and for every life, but its realization depends on a true surrender of my will and your will to Him for the fulfillment of His plan as and where He sees best. He may, however, leave considerable freedom of choice within His moral will, and He may choose to overrule our acknowledged mistakes to fit in with His will, as illustrated in the parable of the potter (Jeremiah 18).

God has a plan for every life. Our circumstances are not accidental but are planned by Him. He is not aiming to produce facsimiles but to develop each personality, so He treats us not as robots but as sons. Sometimes His dealings will seem mysterious at the time, but He has promised a future explanation. Our wisdom and vision are finite, but His are infinite. Because of our limitations there will always be areas we don't understand. For this reason, we need a Guide through the maze of life. "It is not in man to direct his steps" is the dictum of Scripture. We need a guide because the disposition of events is not in our hands. And the upsurge of demonic activity in our day makes His guidance even more necessary.

God has given many promises of personal guidance. If we wish to know what kind of guide He is, we need only look at Christ, who has revealed the Father as a loving, compassionate, gracious, and forgiving God, not as an ascetic ogre whose delight is to say no! If we make a wrong decision, we are not doomed to a second-best life. He delights in giving another chance. (EL)

The True Vine

John 15:7

For a maximum yield, the branches of the vine need heavy pruning—heavier than most other trees. Unless it is severely cut back, the fruit will be sparse and poor. So God prunes the lives of His children, cuts back the undesirable growth of the self-life, not because He delights to see them suffer but that their lives might be increasingly fruitful. He desires to see His children growing in spiritual maturity. There is to be a progression—"fruit, more fruit, much fruit."

The abiding is to be reciprocal: "Abide in me, and I in you" (John 15:4 KJV). There is a conditional promise of answered prayer: "If ye abide in me, and my words abide in you, ye shall ask what ye will, and it shall be done unto you" (v. 7 KJV). Christ in me—I in Christ—Christ's word abiding in me. That is intimacy indeed. With His Word constantly meditated on, loved, believed, and obeyed, we will increasingly receive and reflect the mind of Christ. His will becomes ours, and our desires will be only what He desires.

The little daughter of a friend of mine one day said to her father, "Daddy, I do like to do what I do like to do!" That mutual and reciprocal abiding in Christ will mean that we will like to do what He likes us to do.

Abundant fruit is the proof of discipleship. "My Father is glorified by this, that you bear much fruit, and so prove to be My disciples" (John 15:8 NASB). Not all believers are true disciples, according to that statement. Our discipleship will be displayed by our abiding in His love, enjoying it, reveling in it—a love as great as the Father has for the Son (15:10). Simple obedience is a secret of abiding in His love. Mutuality of love will inevitably result in a deepening intimacy.

Abounding joy results from abiding (15:11 NASB). "I have spoken to you . . . that your joy may be made full"; in other words, "that you may share with Me the joy I possess." Our joy is inextricably linked with His. (EI)

God's Enabling Power

Philippians 4:13

We are not left to our own unaided human resources, dependent on our material environment. The eternal triune God dwells in us. "If a man love me . . . we will come unto him, and make our abode with him." "The Spirit of truth . . . shall be in you" (John 14:23, 17 KJV). There is surely sufficient incentive in this glorious fact to convince the believer to cooperate with his indwelling Guest with all His powers.

Not only does the omnipotent God dwell in the believer's heart, but also He is at work there, the active agent in our sanctification. "It is God which worketh [is working] in you" (Philippians 2:13 KJV) with power adequate for every need. And God's working is always effectual. How impossible it would be for us to force tons of water through solid wood! Yet every day, as the sap rises in the tree, this miracle is performed a thousand times over. With this consciousness of the divine in-working, Paul exclaimed: "I can do all things through Christ which strengtheneth me" (Philippians 4:13 KJV). The words "all things" here do not indicate in the original that he could do "all things in the universe" but implied that he could do everything that was in the good pleasure of God for him to do. Within the sphere of God's will he experienced unlimited power.

"To will and to do of his good pleasure" (Philippians 2:13 KJV). Here is another aspect of the paradox. God works within me to will and to work, and yet the willing and working are mine. But it should be noted that God does not will *instead* of me or work *instead* of me. In sanctification God and I are joined in indivisible partnership, and all efforts to separate the respective spheres of activity are in vain. I will to do, but God works the will in me. I work, but God supplies the power. (SC)

The Law of Restraint

1 Corinthians 11:31

Honest self-criticism should not lead to unwarranted criticism of others but will serve the function of helping to save us from the judgment of God (1 Corinthians 11:31).

Praying Hyde of India learned a lesson that he said was the most profound the Lord ever taught him.

He was burdened about the spiritual condition of a certain pastor and resolved to spend time in intercession for him. He began pouring out his heart for him somewhat as follows: "O God, Thou knowest this brother, how —" He was going to say "cold," when suddenly a hand seemed to be laid on his lips, and a voice said to him in a stern rebuke: "He that toucheth him toucheth the apple of mine eye." A great horror came over Hyde. He had been guilty before God of "accusing the brethren." He had been judging his brother. He fell humbly to his knees.

It was he himself who first needed putting right. He confessed his sin and claimed cleansing. "Whatsoever things . . . are lovely . . . [and] of good report . . . think on these things" (Philippians 4:8 KJV). Then he cried, "Father, show me what things are lovely and of good report in my brother's life."

In a flash he remembered how that pastor had given up all for Christ and endured much suffering. He was reminded of years of hard work, of the tact with which he had managed a difficult congregation, of the many quarrels he had healed, of what a model husband he was. His prayer session was spent in praise for his brother instead of praying for change. (BB)

I Must Choose

Romans 7:18

A. S. Way presents the activity of God as "supplying the impulse, giving you the power to resolve and the will to perform the execution of His good pleasure." We are not cast back upon our own resources. We have the benefits accruing from the death and resurrection of Christ and His gift of the Holy Spirit through whom those benefits become operative in our lives. But I must do the choosing. God does not impart His power or blessings apart from the active participation and cooperation of our wills. Once I put my weak will on God's side and despite my own conscious weakness choose His will, it becomes possible for the Holy Spirit to empower my will.

Even after God has supplied the right impulse, giving humans the power to choose, it still remains for them to act. God cannot act for them. Sanctification is essentially proactive; it does not consist merely in not doing evil things. In exercise of the new power imparted by God's Spirit people are now able to perform "His good pleasure"—the whole will of God. In themselves they are no stronger, but with the divine indwelling and in-working, they are no longer the victim of weakness and sin.

No more apt illustration of the cooperation of man with God is recorded than that of the man with the withered hand. Try as he would, no attempted exercise of his will produced any effect on the paralyzed muscles. When our Lord commanded him to stretch out his hand, a natural reaction would have been for him to say that he had attempted to do so a thousand times, without effect. Was there any reason to expect anything different the thousand-and-first time? But faith had been kindled in the man's heart, and in response to the Lord's command, he exercised his will, and to his joy the paralyzed hand responded, as whole as the other. The activity of faith had released the power of God. The physical realm was affected by the spiritual realm. "All things are possible to him that believeth" (Mark 9:23 KJV). (BB)

The Fire of God

2 Chronicles 7:1

"Now when Solomon had made an end of praying, the fire came down from heaven . . . and the glory of the LORD filled the house" (2 Chronicles 7:1 KJV). The presence of the fire was proof of the presence of God.

Such was the significance of the symbol of fire in Old Testament times. But what is its meaning for us today? In the New Testament it is symbolic of the presence and energy of the Holy Spirit. Announcing the ministry of the Messiah, John the Baptist said, "He shall baptize you with the Holy Ghost, and with fire" (Matthew 3:11 KJV). His prophecy was fulfilled. On the Day of Pentecost when the Holy Spirit came with power upon the assembled disciples, the chosen symbol was prominent. "There appeared unto them cloven tongues like as of fire, and it sat upon each of them" (Acts 2:3 KJV). There is therefore justification for the view that the symbolism of fire in its present-day application is the presence and power of the Holy Spirit.

In Elijah's day the holy fire had disappeared from the altars of Jehovah, and false fire was burning on the altars of Baal. The glory had departed, and no man could rekindle the sacred flame. When Nadab and Abihu "offered strange fire before the LORD" (Numbers 3:4 KJV), they died, for there can be no substitute for the true fire of God.

In our day, the greatest lack in the life of the individual Christian and of the church is the fire of God, the manifested presence and mighty working of the Holy Spirit. There is little about us that cannot be explained on the level of the natural. Our lives are not fire-touched. There is no holy blaze in our churches to which people are irresistibly drawn as a moth to a flame. It is the absence of the fire of God that accounts for the insignificant impact the church is making on a lost world. It never had better organization, more scholarly ministry, greater resources of people and means, and more skillful techniques. And yet never did it make a smaller contribution to solving the problems of a distraught world. Our prayer should be, "Lord, send the fire." What else can meet the need of the hour? (SM)

The Weak Conscience

1 Corinthians 8:10

A *weak* conscience is one that is unhealthy, overscrupulous, and oversensitive (1 Corinthians 8:7–12). It reacts faithfully according to its light, but like a compass with a weak magnetic current, it is easily influenced and tends to vacillate. Its possessor is constantly tormented by doubt as to whether an action is right or wrong and constantly digs up in unbelief what has been sown in faith.

It is very possible to become a martyr to conscience, as John Wesley discovered when he one day vowed that he would not speak to a soul unless the Spirit definitely prompted him. On arriving at Kingswood at the end of the day he found he had not spoken to a soul. He then made the resolution that when there were souls needing speaking to, it would be best for him to do the speaking and trust the Holy Spirit to use the opportunity in the best way.

A conscience may be weak for two reasons—an imperfect knowledge of God's Word and will, with a consequent imperfect faith, or a lack of surrender that leads to vacillating choices. When we obey the known will of God or are willing to do that will, we need not be harassed by an overscrupulous conscience, and we should refuse to constantly review an action committed in good faith. Too many are given to the unsatisfying occupation of photographing themselves and developing their own film. The corrective is to clearly face the issues involved in a situation in the light of Scripture and, seeking the guidance of the Spirit, come to a decision according to one's best judgment. Thereafter we should resolutely refuse to reopen the matter. (SC)

Seen and Unseen

2 Corinthians 4:16–18

"Our inner man is being renewed day by day . . . while we look not at the things which are seen, but at the things which are not seen" (2 Corinthians 4:16–18 NASB). The renewal of the inner man must not be seen as inevitable and automatic. We are being renewed only "while we look . . . at the things which are not seen," the things visible only to the eye of faith. Preoccupation with the visible inhibits the renewal process of the inner man and dims our view of the glory to be revealed.

Concentrated attention and a steadfast gaze are needed to make the invisible real to us. If you wish to see something in the far distance, you alter the focus of your eyes. The process of renewal is operative on our behalf only as we give our undivided attention to eternal things. "Not seen" in this verse means "beyond sight" rather than "invisible," because faith makes these things real. Moses prevailed as he saw Him who is beyond visible sight. His faith brought God and eternal things into the realm of personal experience.

"The things which are seen" seem so solid and satisfying, but in reality they are illusory and transitory. It is "the things which are not seen" that are truly permanent, although they seem so ethereal. Nothing we see with our physical eye is eternal.

A pagan, Andrianus by name, deeply impressed by the fortitude of the persecuted Christians, asked, "What is it which makes these Christians bear these sufferings?" "The unseen things of heaven," was the reply. This was the secret of the radiant and persevering martyrs. Because they had invisible means of support, they were neither cowards nor deserters.

It is impossible to concentrate our entire attention on the seen and the unseen at the same time. It will always be the one at the expense of the other, and we do the choosing. What is the primary focus in our lives, the seen or the unseen? Which exercises the greater influence? When we keep our gaze focused on the unseen and the spiritual, life will not be a reluctant slipping into the tomb but a glorious ascent into the immediate presence of God. (CC)

Valuable Vessels

2 Corinthians 4:7

"We have this treasure in earthen vessels, so that the surpassing greatness of the power will be of God and not from ourselves" (2 Corinthians 4:7 NASB). The roots of missionary passion are concentrated in three words: *Jesus, priceless, treasure.* The *priceless treasure* is described in poetic language in the preceding verse: "The light of the knowledge of the glory of God in the face of Jesus Christ" (4:6 KJV). Our Lord himself affirmed that the good news of the kingdom was a priceless treasure, but in the ultimate sense it is Christ himself. The treasure is not a way of life to embrace but a Person to adore. But we have lost the wonder of it all. Imagine the excitement of the farmer of whom Jesus spoke, when his plow unearthed the hidden treasure! We must recapture the wonder of "Jesus, priceless treasure."

Paul sets in contrast *the contemptible vessel,* as though to highlight the contrast of such precious treasure being housed in so commonplace a vessel, yet this was God's appointed method and Christ's chosen role. He chose to share with us the limitations of our physical body, our "house of clay." That earthen vessel was the repository of "all the treasures of wisdom and knowledge" (Colossians 2:3 KJV) and "all the fulness of the Godhead bodily" (Colossians 2:9 KJV). God was pleased to display His most precious jewel in a setting of common clay. This gives a unique dignity to the vessel. Who are we to be worthy recipients of such honor?

Despite its privilege, the earthen vessel remains weak and easily corrupted. Paul knew that it was the breaking of the earthen vessel of Christ's body that enabled the full light of the knowledge of the glory of God to blaze forth to others, and the principle is the same for His disciples. It is enough to satisfy the servant that he be in the image of his Lord.

It is the strategy of God that our human weakness should be a backdrop for the display of His divine power. "The exceeding greatness of his power" (Ephesians 1:19 KJV) is to be seen as coming from God, and not from us. It is a comforting thought that God does not use us merely in spite of our weakness, but actually because of it. (CC)

The Gift of the Spirit

1 Corinthians 12:1, 11

"Now concerning spiritual gifts . . . all these worketh that one and the selfsame Spirit, dividing to every man severally as he will" (1 Corinthians 12:1, 11 KJV). God has given us two unspeakable gifts—His Son and His Spirit. One is the source of our salvation, the other the inspirer of our service.

A clear distinction, however, must be made between the *gift* of the Spirit and the *gifts* of the Spirit. The former was bestowed on the church in fulfillment of the promise of the Father and in answer to the prayer of Christ. The latter are given to individual believers as and when the Holy Spirit in His sovereignty chooses.

On the Day of Pentecost, fifty days after the crucifixion, the great gift of the Spirit was poured on the waiting Jewish Christians. Later, in the house of Cornelius, the Gentiles too became beneficiaries. The gift of the Spirit is for every member of the body of Christ without discrimination. The gifts of the Spirit are special and bestowed individually. The gift is absolute and permanent, but the gifts may atrophy through disuse.

Our hymnology is often faulty in petitioning God to give His Spirit, as though He had never been given. We rightly pray for a greater manifestation of His power in our lives and service, but the gift has already been made to all, once and for all.

Every believer has been granted some spiritual gift (1 Corinthians 12:11), but not all have tried to discover what their particular gift is. "Every man hath his proper gift of God" (1 Corinthians 7:7 KJV), the one most suited and essential to his function in the church. No one may demand specific gifts, for the Spirit is sovereign and gives "as he will."

A spiritual gift is bestowed apart from merit and qualifies its possessor for some form of spiritual service. There is unity without uniformity—"diversities of gifts, but the same Spirit" (1 Corinthians 12:4 KJV). Not all are clearly visible, as, for example, the gift of "helps," but all contribute to the upbuilding of the church. Some of the hidden parts of the body are the most essential.

Paul exhorts us to "covet earnestly the best gifts" (1 Corinthians 12:31 KJV), those most calculated to help and edify others. (CC)

Dealing with Doubt

Matthew 12:39

There is much we may learn from Thomas's experience about the Master's method of dealing with doubting hearts. No believer is immune to the ravages of doubt. Even after having genuinely believed, it is still possible for us to have intellectual problems. But Jesus did not exclude this doubter from the rank of the apostles. Nor did He blame him for having a skeptical disposition. The Lord did not scold him for desiring satisfying evidence on which to base his faith, for He knew it was not the unbelief of the atheist or agnostic but the doubt of a soul genuinely searching. Archbishop William Temple suggests: "Such vigour of disbelief plainly represents a strong urge to believe, held down by common sense and its habitual dread of disillusionment."

There is a world of difference between "an evil heart of unbelief" (Hebrews 3:12 KJV) and the doubts of one who is weak in faith, between arrogant unbelief and the sensitive questioning of an earnest but hesitant heart. The doubting of the latter is a regrettable infirmity, but that of the former is an affront to God.

When the unbelieving Pharisees demanded a sign, Jesus promptly refused. "An evil and adulterous generation craves for a sign; and yet no sign will be given to it but the sign of Jonah the prophet" (Matthew 12:39 NASB). But when Thomas wanted not only to hear but also to see and feel truth, Jesus graciously met him in his infirmity.

The beatitude Jesus talked about regarding sightless faith was not suggesting gullibility. He did not endorse a belief without inquiry and consideration, but He did indicate the necessity of a leap of faith. If it were asked what Jesus meant by believing without seeing, the answer probably is not to be found with absolute demonstration of proof. In other words, it means being willing to take the final leap of faith in the risen and living Christ.

It remains to be said that, as in the case of Thomas, God overrules doubt once and for all. It was due to Thomas's unbelief that the Lord spoke of the ninth beatitude. When those who doubt do come to faith, they believe even more firmly what they once doubted. (JL)

Slaves Set Free

Romans 6:22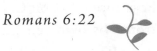

The liberation of the will from the thralldom of sin brings with it the corresponding desire for the will of God alone.

When Abraham Lincoln affixed his signature to the historic Emancipation Proclamation, every slave in the United States of America was immediately and automatically released from slavery. From the moment the ink was dry on the document, every slave was potentially free. But that did not mean that every slave immediately enjoyed actual liberty. Some masters deliberately concealed from the slaves the news of their emancipation.

Before they experienced their freedom, the slaves first had to *hear* the good news. Then they had to *believe* that joyous news, even though it seemed too good to be true. Next they had to *reckon* on the facts being true, not of slaves in general, but of themselves in particular. But they could do all this and still remain slaves. They had to *assert* their freedom and *refuse* any longer to remain in bondage to their former masters. In doing this, they could count on the whole might of the United States being behind them.

So must it be with us. We have learned from the Holy Scriptures that on Calvary Christ signed in blood drawn from His own veins an emancipation proclamation that potentially freed all believers from the dominion of sin. It now remains for us to *believe* that fact, to *reckon* it as being true in our case, and then to act on it, *refusing* any longer to be slaves of sin. When we dare to do this, we will find that all the might of the risen Son of God is on our side, and we will be free indeed. Sin will be powerless to bring us again under its sway and dominion. (SP)

The Likeness of Christ

2 Corinthians 3:18

"But we all . . . beholding as in a mirror the glory of the Lord, are being transformed into the same image from glory to glory, just as from the Lord, the Spirit" (2 Corinthians 3:18 NASB). Transformation into the likeness of Christ is not the result of painful striving against the bad things that captivate the heart but the result of a yearning desire for the glory of the Lord. This was the most important aspect in the new covenant of which Paul is speaking in this chapter. The old covenant only brings about deeper despair, but the new covenant holds out the attractive possibility of an attainable likeness to Christ.

The transformation begins with an objective vision of the glory of the Lord, not with mere subjective introspection. But where may this captivating vision be seen? Not in the illuminated heavens, but in the illuminated mirror of the Word. There we see reflected "the glory of God in the face of Jesus Christ" (4:6 KJV). The glory is, of course, His attributes of character and conduct and His revealed divinity. The Jews saw the face but missed the glory because of the veil of prejudice and disobedience. The vision comes as the reward of prolonged contemplation and prayer.

The objective vision of Christ results in a subjective transformation—"we are being transformed." God is not satisfied with us as we are, nor are we satisfied with ourselves. His purpose is to refashion us in the image of the Son in whom He found such delight. We have no inherent glory, but this transformation will make us reflectors of His glory. God's plan is not for a mere outward imitation of Christ but inward transformation into His image. Mose's face reflected God's glory, but the glory was external and transient. This is an ever-increasing glory that we internalize and keep for eternity.

Who is the transforming agent? "The Lord, the Spirit." The change is not automatic—our part is to steadfastly gaze on Christ as He is revealed in Scripture and to exercise an expectant faith in the Spirit's operation. He affects the change. As we meditate on our beloved Lord, coveting the beauties of His character, the Holy Spirit is working in us the virtues and graces that dwell in fullness in Him. Beholding Him, we are changed. (CC)

Simple Obedience

Acts 5:29

I t is well to remember that a great many matters that call for our decision are already taken care of. The sphere in which we have to decide is not so large as we may think, but it does include some very crucial issues.

Consider these areas in which it is not prayer for guidance that is required, but simple obedience:

Clear, unequivocal statements of scriptural principle. The Bible gives general guidance on all matters of morals, ethics, spiritual life, family life, and church life. The question we have to answer is, "What does the Bible have to say in principle or by example on this subject?"

Claims of duty. Relationships impose duties. We have fundamental duties in the areas of family, business, profession, church, and community. There will be minor decisions to make within the scope of particular fundamental duties. For example, parents have a fundamental responsibility to provide for their children, but that will involve many minor decisions. The question to answer is, "Where does my duty lie?" This will take care of a surprising number of decisions.

Obedience to constituted authority. Our Lord has told us, "Give back to Caesar what is Caesar's, and to God what is God's" (Matthew 22:21). In writing to the Roman Christians, Paul said, "Let everyone be subject to the governing authorities, for there is no authority except that which God has established. The authorities that exist have been established by God" (Romans 13:1–2). This injunction is clear, but there is one more question that calls for an answer when we face decisions: "Does this law or civic responsibility contravene the law of God?" If it does, then our attitude should be the same as that of the apostles: "We must obey God rather than human beings!" (Acts 5:29). (EL)

Intimacy through Growing Love

Philippians 3:7–8

In His memorable private discussion with Peter after his denial, the Lord made it clear to His penitent friend that the future would require of Peter an unwavering devotion to himself. Three times He probed Peter's conscience to its depths with the searching query, "Simon son of John, do you love me?" (John 21:15–17). He knew that if Peter gave Him his unqualified love and devotion, he could then be entrusted as a spiritual shepherd with the sensitive task of strengthening his brethren. Increasing intimacy would develop only through growing love.

Paul's experience of intimacy with Christ only fed the flames of a passion to know Him still better: "That I may know Him and the power of His resurrection and the fellowship of His sufferings, being conformed to His death" (Philippians 3:10 NASB).

Paul had been assuring the believers at Philippi that his deepest concern was not his ancestry, achievements, or prestige, but the attaining of a deeper fellowship with his Lord. "But whatever things were gain to me, those things I have counted as loss for the sake of Christ. More than that, I count all things to be loss in view of the surpassing value of knowing Christ Jesus my Lord, for whom I have suffered the loss of all things, and count them but rubbish so that I may gain Christ" (Philippians 3:7–8 NASB). For such an inestimable reward, no price was too great.

All spiritual ministry flows from the reality of our knowledge of God and the vitality of our fellowship with Him and His Son. A successful, fruitful ministry does not just happen—it is purchased by surrender of all we possess. The more influential the ministry is, the steeper the price will be. It cannot be paid in a lump sum; we pay for it in gradually increasing installments as the challenges increase. There is no such thing as a cheap, fruitful ministry. (EI)

Steps in Discerning God's Will

Romans 14:22–23

B e unconditionally willing to do it, whatever it is. It may be that your will needs to be redirected. Be willing to be made willing.

- Be obedient to any light the Lord has already given. If you are not obeying that, why expect more?
- Be patient. The road ahead may not be revealed all at once; it seldom is. But God will show you each step as you need to take it. We sing the hymn "One Step Enough for Me" but don't always mean it.
- Remember the intellectual component in this exercise. John Wesley maintained, "God generally guides me by presenting reasons to my mind for acting in a certain way"—not feelings to my heart.
- Gather all the information you can about the options that are open to you.
- Seek advice from your Christian parents, your pastor, or a trusted Christian counselor. However, don't allow them to make the decision for you.

It is your life that is at stake, and you will have to live with the consequences of that decision.

- Ensure that the course you propose to pursue is biblically legitimate. Submit it to the test of Scripture.
- List the pros and cons of the course you propose, and as you weigh them, ask the Holy Spirit to sway your mind in the direction of His will, believing that He does it in keeping with James 1:5.
- Don't ask for extraordinary guidance, for that is the exception and not the rule, especially as you mature spiritually. Spectacular signs are given only by the sovereign choice of God. Faith is content with quiet guidance.
- Make the best decision you can in light of the facts, believing God has answered your prayer for wisdom.
- Expect the witness of the Spirit in a deepening conviction that this is the will of God for you. Circumstances may confirm your guidance. (EL)

Greater Fruitfulness

Isaiah 28:24

The loving heavenly Father can be trusted in the adaptation, timing, and duration of the discipline His love permits. We are safe in His hands.

The discipline is always preparatory to blessing and can bring nothing but blessing when rightly received. It is here that our responsibility lies. Food not digested is a discomfort, not a blessing. Disciplines not rightly received sour rather than sweeten the character. To ask "Why?" when the chastening stroke falls is in effect to charge the all-wise and all-loving God with being harsh. He does not rend the heart merely to demonstrate His power and sovereignty but to prepare us for greater fruitfulness. He prunes every branch that does bear fruit to increase its yield. The discipline is lovingly purposeful. How do we react to God's plow? Does it soften, subdue, or chasten us? Or does it harden and stiffen our resistance to His will? Does it sweeten or sour us?

Our reaction to family problems and financial reverses, to suffering and disappointment, to thwarted ambitions and disappointed expectations is all-important. If we submit, feeling that resistance is counterproductive, that is better than continued rebellion. If we respond to God's dealings glumly, that is still attaining higher ground. But it is when we embrace God's unexplained difficult providences with a song that God is most glorified and we are most blessed. When Samuel Rutherford lay in Aberdeen prison, he used to write at the top of his letters, "God's Palace, Aberdeen."

Madame Guyon, a cultured Frenchwoman, was imprisoned for her faith from 1695 to 1705. Instead of complaining at her lot, she joyously accepted God's will as her gift from Him. "While I was a prisoner in Vincennes," she wrote, "I passed my time in great peace. I sang songs of joy which the maid who served me learned by heart as fast as I made them. And we together sang Thy praises, O my God. The stones of my prison walls shone like rubies in my eyes. My heart was full of that joy which Thou givest to them that love Thee in the midst of their greatest crosses." (SM)

Life Is a Tapestry

Genesis 50:20

The experiences of life when taken in isolation may seem anything but good, but blended together the result is only good.

In adverse circumstances unbelief asks, "How can this be working for good?" The answer is, "Wait until the Great Physician has finished writing the prescription." Who cannot look back on life to see that things considered disastrous proved in the ultimate to be blessings in disguise? An artist blends colors that to the unskilled eye seem far removed from the objective. But wait until she has finished her mixing.

Life has been likened to an elaborate tapestry being woven on the loom. For the beauty of the pattern it is imperative that the colors must not be all of the same hue. Some must be bright and beautiful, others dark and somber. It is as they are all worked together that they contribute to the beauty of the pattern.

In time of severe trial there is always the temptation, while assenting to the truth in general, to feel that our present circumstances are an exception. If that were so, the text is untrue, and the truth of the overruling providence of God in the affairs of humanity has no meaning.

As tragedy upon tragedy overwhelmed Joseph—banishment from home, sale as a slave, unjust imprisonment—it was difficult for him to see these untoward events working together for his good. Yet in retrospect he said to his brothers, "But as for you, ye thought evil against me; but God meant it unto good" (Genesis 50:20 KJV).

In the events of life God has an end in view that is worthy of Him and will bring about our fullest praise and thanksgiving when we cease to know in part. Even if called upon to face the wrath of humans or Devil, we can confidently rest in the assurance that it will ultimately result in praise to God, and that which cannot do so will be restrained. (SM)

The Purpose of Life

2 Timothy 4:6–8

M any people, young and old, are frankly disappointed with life. It has not given them what they have craved, and they are disillusioned and frustrated. The French philosopher Goethe said: "I have been deemed, and I believe justly, one of fortune's favorites. Yet I cannot, as I look back on my life, recall more than three weeks of positive happiness in the whole." This may be rather an extreme case, and yet it is by no means an isolated one. A whole generation of young people could make a similar confession.

By way of contrast, hear Paul's testimony: "I am now ready to be offered, and the time of my departure is at hand. I have fought a good fight, I have finished my course, I have kept the faith: Henceforth there is laid up for me a crown of righteousness, which the Lord, the righteous judge, shall give me at that day" (2 Timothy 4:6–8 KJV). There is no disillusionment or frustration here. He had lived life to the full, had worked hard and suffered much, but at the end he found satisfaction, fulfillment, and reward.

If Paul were challenged and asked what made him what he was and what had enabled him to triumph in such painful and adverse circumstances, he might have replied: "Once I could describe my life like this: For me to live is Paul. But since I saw the vision on the Damascus road, the center of my life has shifted. Now for me to live is Christ." To him life was now someone else.

It is a searching spiritual exercise to examine your life and finish Paul's statement for yourself: "To me to live is _____." There must be some center, some unifying motive to our lives. What is it: self or Christ? Here Paul was saying that since his conversion, the center of life had shifted from him to someone else, and that change had altered the circumference (or circumstances) of his life as well. (BB)

A Vision of God and Oneself

Isaiah 5:23

The vision of God inevitably results in a vision of oneself and a sense of unworthiness and impurity. The beatific vision deflated Moses. It caused Daniel to see the corruption, not of his vices only but of what he had considered his virtues. It blinded Saul. It threw John on his face before the angel. It punctured Isaiah's complacency.

We all instinctively shrink from the embarrassment of this personal vision. We tend to react adversely to preachers whose message has a subjective edge to it pointing at us, because it seems to downgrade our self-esteem. We much prefer an objective message that does not expose us to our true selves. But God is not so lenient. If we allow Him, He will ruthlessly strip away all camouflage concealing our sins, both conscious and unconscious, and reveal us to ourselves as He sees us.

In light of this, there was the collapse of Isaiah's complacency: "Woe to me ... I am ruined!" Isaiah was no lukewarm prophet. Indeed, judged by human standards he was probably the most upright man in the nation. Like Paul, in the sight of the Law he would be blameless. But when he came into the dazzling whiteness of God's holiness, all he could do was to utter the cry of the leper: "Unclean, unclean!" He saw that God was eternally opposed to all that was evil, even in those who claimed an intimate relationship with Him.

The contemporary philosophy is to say that our greatest need is more self-reliance and self-confidence. If we are to judge by Isaiah's experience, God indicates that our greatest need is self-abasement and a deep sense of insufficiency that will cast us back on Him. (BF)

Cleansing by the Blood

1 John 2:1

The record of the Passover night in Exodus 12 represents the blood of the innocent victim applied in faith as availing to hold back the execution of judgment on the Israelites. Because of the blood, the avenger becomes the protector.

Another twofold picture is presented in Leviticus 16, which details the ritual of the great Day of Atonement. The death of Christ is there represented as both satisfying the righteous claims of God against the sinning person and forever bearing away his or her polluted sins "unto a land not inhabited" (v. 22 KJV).

In Numbers 19, read in conjunction with Hebrews 9:13–14, we are introduced to Christ's death as a continual provision for the constant cleansing of Christians as they walk amid the inescapable impurities of their daily life. It is God's provision for the maintenance of unbroken communion with Him. Sins of the future are in view as well as sins of the past and sins of which we are unconscious as well as those of which we are conscious.

There is no possibility of forsaking sin entirely. But we have the power over sin. This harmonizes entirely with

Paul's question and answer, "Shall we continue in sin ... God forbid" (Romans 6:1–2 KJV). The objectives John had in view for the believers were clearly expressed: "My little children, these things write I unto you, that ye sin not" (1 John 2:1 KJV). But in the same passage, he recognizes the possibility of sinning and reveals the remedy for such a condition. Sinning is no longer necessary, but it is possible and therefore must be provided for. The lifeboat is provided, not because the vessel must sink, but in case it does. The work of Christ under consideration was such a divine provision. It is one of the richest in spiritual teaching of the Old Testament types and will amply repay close study, for Paul assures us that "all these things happened unto them for examples: and they are written for our admonition, upon whom the ends of the world are come" (1 Corinthians 10:11 KJV). (SP)

Loyalty to the Master

Matthew 5:11

Why did our Lord make His terms of discipleship so exacting, when the inevitable result would be the loss of popular support? It was because He was concerned more with quality than with quantity. He desired a band of chosen men and women, a Gideon's band, on whose unwavering devotion He could count in days of crisis. He wanted trustworthy disciples on whom He could rely when building His church or battling with the powers of evil (Luke 14:29, 31). Once disciples are convinced of the majesty and the glory of the Christ they follow and of the cause in which they are enlisted, they will be willing for any sacrifice.

Several centuries ago an invading Eastern king, whose march had met with unbroken success, neared the territory of the young chieftain Abu Taber. Hearing of his valor, the king was reluctant to kill him and instead sent an ambassador with terms of peace. When he heard the proposal, Abu Taber summoned one of his soldiers, handed him a dagger, and commanded, "Plunge this into your breast." The soldier obeyed and fell dead at his feet. Calling another, he ordered, "Leap over that precipice into the Euphrates." Without a moment's hesitation he leaped to his death. Turning to the ambassador Abu said, "Go, tell your master I have five hundred men like that, and within twenty-four hours I will have him chained with my dogs." The king with his greatly superior numbers continued his advance, but numbers were of no avail against the fierce loyalty of Abu Taber's devotees. Before a day had passed, the king was chained with Abu's dogs. It is the quality of loyalty that is important.

Christianity truly interpreted has never been popular. Indeed, a religion that is popular is far removed from the teaching of our Lord. "Woe unto you, when all men shall speak well of you! for so did their fathers to the false prophets," He warned (Luke 6:26 KJV). On the contrary, Christians are truly blessed when people revile them and say all manner of evil against them falsely for Christ's sake (Matthew 5:11). We are invited to share not His popularity, but His unpopularity. (SM)

Inward Renewal

2 Corinthians 4:16–18

Therefore we do not lose heart, but though our outer man is decaying, yet our inner man is being renewed day by day. For momentary, light affliction is producing for us an eternal weight of glory far beyond all comparison, while we look not at the things which are seen, but at the things which are not seen; for the things which are seen are temporal, but the things which are not seen are eternal. (2 Corinthians 4:16–18 NASB)

The paragraph in which this text occurs balances six pairs of words: *outer* and *inner, decaying* and *renewed, light* and *weight, affliction* and *glory, seen* and *not seen, temporal* and *eternal*. Here is one of Paul's great secrets—the prescription for weakness is suffering. He well knew the peril of a spiritual wound on the battlefield, so he shares his own experience of God's upholding power with the Corinthian believers.

Actually, the expression "we do not lose heart" is derived from military life and could be rendered "we do not act as deserters and cowards." We do not walk away from positions of trust even if they are dangerous, because we look to the glory ahead.

It is true that the outer man, which belongs to this temporal world, is decaying and suffers wear and tear. With advancing years, physical vigor wanes and beauty fades. Old age and death advance with a relentless step, and those whose lives are governed only by sight and time are weighed down and depleted. But "we do not lose heart," as Paul states.

Here is the blessed paradox: our outer man is *decaying*; our inner man is *renewed*. The inner man is rejuvenated in the "divine beauty parlor" by the Holy Spirit. Each new day brings a fresh provision of divine strength. What a cheering revelation from Paul! By a divine alchemy, God harnesses the very forces that destroy the outer person to develop the inner person. And this renewal goes on day by day. There are no idle days with the Holy Spirit!

This was the reason Paul was able to view with a larger perspective the wasting away of his outer man through persecution, disease, and innumerable hardships. It enabled him to make the incredible statement, "[I] glory in tribulations" (Romans 5:3 KJV), because he knew that the Holy Spirit used these experiences to mature him and to strengthen his inner man. (CC)

The Spirit Helps Us

Galatians 4:6

The Spirit himself leads us into the presence of the Father. "For through him we ... have access to the Father by one Spirit" (Ephesians 2:18). The picture behind *access* is that of a court official introducing people who desire an audience with the king. This is exactly what the Spirit does for us.

As the "spirit of grace and supplication" (Zechariah 12:10), He overcomes our reluctance, working in us the desire to pray. He graciously, yet faithfully, reveals to us our true heart-needs, and He leads us to seek their fulfillment in prayer.

He imparts an assurance in worship and a receptivity that creates freedom and confidence in the presence of God. "God sent the Spirit of his Son into our hearts, the Spirit who calls out, '*Abba* Father'" (Galatians 4:6). Children are uninhibited in the presence of an understanding and loving father, and so may we be in our prayers to our heavenly Father.

He helps us in the ignorance of our minds and in the weakness of our bodies, as well as in the sickness of the soul. "In the same way, the Spirit helps us in our weakness. We do not know what we ought to pray for" (Romans 8:26), or as it is in the King James Version, "We know not what we should pray for as we ought."

We can count on the Spirit's aid in guiding us into the will of God by illuminating Scripture to us and by stimulating and directing our mental processes. He purifies our desires and redirects them toward the will of God, for He alone knows and can interpret God's will and purpose. "No one knows the thoughts of God except the Spirit of God" (1 Corinthians 2:11). He also increases our motivation and inspires confidence and faith in a loving Father. (PP)

Answers to Temptation

Matthew 4:10

Because the Christ to whom we are united by faith was victorious over every type of temptation by Satan, we may share in His triumph as we appropriate it by faith.

Here is the essence of the three temptations:

1. The first was the temptation to satisfy a legitimate appetite by illegitimate means.

2. The second was the temptation to produce spiritual results by unspiritual means.

3. The third was the temptation to obtain a lawful heritage by unlawful means.

It is significant that each of Jesus's answers to Satan was a quotation from the book of Deuteronomy. Our Lord thus confirmed the Pentateuch as the Word of God.

Joseph Parker draws attention to some interesting features in our Lord's answers to Satan's suggestions.

- They were not the result of Christ's divine keen intellect that is above and beyond what we sinful humans may claim.

- They were not the outcome of ready wit nor of an unexpected flash of inspiration.

- They do not bear the marks of inventive genius.

- They were not answers that came on the spur of the moment as a result of His infinite wisdom. They were not philosophical arguments elaborately stated and eloquently discussed. *But* they were simple enough for the average child to understand. They were quotations from the Word of God on which He meditated day and night. Only the eternal, all-powerful Word of God will cause Satan to flee defeated. Human reasoning and arguments are weak in conflicts with Satan because they lack authority. (31 Days)

Warfare and Weapons

2 Corinthians 10:3–4

"Though we walk in the flesh, we do not war according to the flesh, for the weapons of our warfare are not of the flesh, but divinely powerful for the destruction of fortresses" (2 Corinthians 10:3–4 NASB). The reality of the spiritual battle, of which we are very aware on a daily basis, proves the existence of Satan. The fierceness of the fight demonstrates the power and tenacity of the foe.

The warfare is spiritual, not waged in the flesh but conducted on the spiritual level; this is in a different realm from where the unregenerate person lives. It is *intangible* warfare, not with physical weapons. We cannot seize people and drag them from Satan's grasp. We can reach and deliver them only through spiritual tactics. It is a battle of two armies with entirely different goals.

It is also *interminable* warfare. The war that began in Eden will end only when Satan is finally bound. In the meantime, he is struggling unceasingly to gain control of the world and its inhabitants. There is no escaping the effects of this warfare.

The battlefield is the human mind, in our imaginations and thoughts (v. 5). Battles always have their focal points, and this war is waged in the realm of our thoughts. *Imagination,* in this instance, means speculations apart from God for our own benefit. The imagination in this unhealthy sense is the source of a great deal of our sin. It conjures up wrong images and desires, and when the will entertains instead of rejects them, the citadel falls. *Thoughts* include our independent plans and purposes. The thoughts and purposes of the unregenerate man are contrary to those of God.

The invincible weapons at our disposal are the cross and the Word of Truth. "They overcame him by the blood of the Lamb, and by the word of their testimony" (Revelation 12:11 KJV). We need to use them both in the power of the Spirit. (CC)

The Ape of God

Revelation 16:13

It was St. Augustine who called the devil *Simius Dei*, the ape, the imitator, of God. This concept finds support in Paul's warning in 2 Corinthians: "For such men are false apostles, deceitful workers, disguising themselves as apostles of Christ. No wonder, for even Satan disguises himself as an angel of light" (11:13–14 NASB).

In Revelation 13:11 John writes, "Then I saw a second beast, coming out of the earth. It had two horns like a lamb, but it spoke like a dragon." The identity of the beast is clear from the context. The dragon apes the lamb. Satan imitates God. He sets up his own counterfeit religious system in imitation of Christianity.

Satan has his own trinity—the dragon, the beast, and the false prophet (Revelation 16:13). He has his own church, "a synagogue of Satan" (Revelation 2:9). He has his own ministers (2 Corinthians 11:4–5). He has formulated his own system of theology, "doctrines of demons" (1 Timothy 4:1 NASB). He has established his own sacrificial system, "the sacrifices of pagans are offered to demons" (1 Corinthians 10:20). He has his own communion service, "the cup of demons... and the table of demons" (1 Corinthians 10:21). His ministers proclaim his own gospel, "a gospel other than the one we preached to you" (Galatians 1:8). He has his own throne (Revelation 13:2) as well as his own worshipers (Revelation 13:4).

So he has developed a thorough imitation of Christianity, viewed as a system of religion. In his role as the imitator of God, he inspires false christs, self-constituted messiahs (Matthew 24:4–5). He employs false teachers who are specialists in his "theology," to bring in "destructive heresies, even denying the sovereign Lord who bought them" (2 Peter 2:1). They are adept at mixing truth and error in such proportions as to make error palatable. They carry on their teaching disguised as truth, but in fact twist all that is good and holy. (SN)

Consecrated for Service

Philippians 2:12–13

I s it possible that we may be holding back our lives from the living God because of fear of what it might cost? Dr. Alexander Maclaren said the meaning of being a Christian is that, in response to the gift of a whole Christ, a person gives his or her whole self to Him.

It is a life separated to the glory of God. Inherent in the word *consecration* is the idea of separateness. There must of necessity be separation from sin if there is to be separation to God. "Having therefore these promises . . . let us cleanse ourselves from all filthiness of the flesh and spirit" is Paul's exhortation (2 Corinthians 7:1 KJV). Here again *cleanse* implies a definite, deliberate act. We can renounce everything we know to be wrong by a resolute act of our renewed wills, reinforced by the Holy Spirit (Philippians 2:12–13).

But the separation meant here is not the separation found in the monastery. It is *insulation* from what is sinful rather than *isolation* from it. We have to go on living in a sinful world among sinful people. It is not merely avoiding negative things. Consecrated Christians hate evil, but they have a passion for the right and for the glory of God and Christ. They test all their actions by the one standard: "Is this for the glory of God?" They will do anything, suffer anything, if only God is glorified. Nothing is too costly to give to the Master. Sacrifice has been described as the ecstasy of giving the best we have to the One we love the most.

Then it is a life concentrated on the service of God. Robert Lee tells of a convert who was testifying to the fact that the Lord had helped him along the line of consecration. But he had not gotten the word correctly. He said it two or three times like this: "I'm so glad He helped me to be wholly concentrated unto Him." He may have used the wrong word, but he expressed the right idea.

Consecration will always end in concentration on God and His service. It is not an end in itself. If it does not find expression in holy activity, it is superficial. (BB)

Fear Him Who Destroys

Luke 19:10

O ur Lord affirmed that the fundamental purpose of His coming was "to seek and to save that which was lost" (Luke 19:10 KJV). What is the meaning of that term as He used it? Its serious implications are seen in the fact that it is the same word as "perish" in John 3:16 and "destroy" in Matthew 10:28 (KJV). "Fear him which is able to destroy both soul and body in hell." The idea behind this is not "abolition of existence" but "waste" and "ruin."

In the threefold parable of Luke 15, Jesus used the illustration of the lost coin, the lost sheep, and the lost son. The coin was carelessly lost; the sheep was heedlessly lost; the son was willfully lost. But each was still lost and required to be found by someone else (vv. 4, 8, 32). Being lost is the antithesis of the blessedness implied in the word *saved* in its widest meaning. It is a term that describes not only a present condition and a sinful character but also a coming disaster in which all unregenerate people are involved. "The Lord Jesus shall be revealed from heaven with his mighty angels, in flaming fire taking vengeance on them that know not God, and that obey not the gospel of our Lord Jesus Christ:

who shall be punished with everlasting destruction from the presence of the Lord, and from the glory of his power" (2 Thessalonians 1:7–9 KJV). In His atoning death Christ had in view, not merely the improvement of people's personal and social conditions, but their salvation from both a sinful state and an awful destiny.

It should be noted that it is not those who hear of Christ and reject Him, as distinct from those who have never had a chance, who are lost. Jesus came to save those who were *already* lost, who were "condemned already" (John 3:18 KJV). Paul wrote, "If our gospel be hid, it is hid to them that are lost" (2 Corinthians 4:3 KJV)—not merely in danger of being lost but already lost in their separation from God. People do not need to wait until they die to perish. Death will only make visible in the final state of life what is already a fact in this life. (HL)

PART 2

LORD
OF THE
EVERYDAY

Instruction for Converts

Romans 10:9–10

Many promising converts have made little progress in the new life of the Spirit simply because they were not correctly instructed at the time of their conversion. It is not wise to overload newborn babes with sage advice, but several things should be made crystal clear to them.

- To be happy, Christians must confess Christ to others at the earliest possible moment, preferably to their own family and circle of friends first and then to their workmates (Romans 10:9, 10). They must be out to experience God's best for their life. Would-be secret disciples never know the real joy of the Lord. Explain that if they trust their newly found Savior, He will give them the power to testify on His behalf (Philippians 4:13).

- Show them that Christ is not only their Savior but their Lord (Romans 10:9) and that therefore their will must be fully surrendered to their Master.

- Urge them to read the Bible every day, first thing in the morning if possible, and ask the Holy Spirit to make the Bible come alive to them. Explain that the Bible is to the spiritual life what bread is to the physical life and that they cannot grow spiritually without "food."

- Having heard God's voice in the Bible, new converts should be instructed to let God hear their voice in prayer, to pour out their soul and their desires before God (Matthew 6:6). Make clear that it is their privilege to talk with God and walk with God every hour of the day and to claim the fulfillment of His promises. Encourage the habit of spontaneous prayer throughout the day as well as quality time spent in solitude with God.

- Advise them to begin to work diligently for Christ and seek to win others to Him. (DA)

Praying for Rulers

1 Timothy 2:12

"I urge . . . that petitions, prayers, intercession and thanksgiving be made for all people—for kings and all those in authority, that we may live peaceful and quiet lives in all godliness and holiness" (1 Timothy 2:1–2). Christians have civic and national as well as spiritual responsibilities, and, among other ways, we are to discharge these responsibilities in prayer. We should pray for those who hold civic office and national or international offices on all levels. Are we discharging our responsibilities in this area? Is it any wonder that the voice of the church is so muted and her influence so minimal in the affairs of the world when she neglects this primary and divinely ordained method of influencing national and world affairs? If prayer cannot influence the course of world events, Paul's exhortation is pointless.

Scripture teaches that the church and the Christian owe a duty to the state beyond mere payment of taxes and obedience to laws. It matters not whether rulers are good or bad; we are under obligation to pray for them as they exercise their offices. It is instructive to note that the ruler in Rome when Paul penned this letter to Timothy was the infamous Nero.

Rulers may be persecutors or dictators, but Christians are not to stop praying for them.

In general, the early Christians did not evade or ignore their divinely imposed civic and national responsibilities. One of the early Fathers, Tertullian, gives us a glimpse into their practice: "We pray for ourselves, for the state of the world, for the peace of all things, and for the postponement of the end."

Public officials have heavy burdens to bear, and they wield far-reaching influence. Their decisions affect the church, the city, and the nation. We must realize that the deeds of wicked people and corrupt officials can be held in check by our prayers.

In the midst of toppling thrones, Daniel maintained his serenity because he knew there was a sovereign God in heaven to whom he could pray. For him, that canceled every adverse factor. He could defy the decree of the ruler of Babylon, for he knew that "the Most High is sovereign over all kingdoms on earth and gives them to anyone he wishes" (Daniel 4:17). (PP)

In the Father's Hands

Mark 11:24

W e can be assured that we will receive all that God is willing to consistently grant us when we have prayed the prayer of faith in accordance with Mark 11:24. We can rest assured that He will exercise His divine influence on those who are the subjects of our prayers. He will do this to the fullest possible extent, short of encroaching on their free wills, so as to enable them to come to Christ or to otherwise conform to His will. We can be sure that He will choose the best time and employ the best methods to make His influence felt.

But what if the prayer does not seem to be answered, in spite of the sincerity of our desires and the earnestness of our pleas? Some light is thrown on our perplexity by the fact that our Lord himself had to face the same problem. He did not see His heart's desire for humanity realized in every case. There were those over whom He had to utter the lament of unfulfilled love: "Jerusalem, Jerusalem ... how often I have longed to gather your children together, as a hen gathers her chicks under her wings, and you were not willing"

(Luke 13:34). And on another occasion He had to mourn, "You refuse to come to me to have life" (John 5:40).

No accusation about failure in prayer or about lack of true concern for the people being prayed for could be laid at His door, as it can all too often be laid at ours. But in spite of this, sometimes His prayers were not answered immediately or in the way we would expect. Yet He refused to exercise His divine power in order to compel people to come to Him. This is what is involved in the solemn responsibility of being human. We can say no to God.

However, this did not discourage Jesus from praying. He recognized the solemn fact, as we must, that in the final analysis the human will can become so debased that it can thwart the loving desires of God's heart. In the face of those circumstances, He did what we must do. He prayed and trustingly left the issue in the hands of His Father. (PP)

Restoring Relationships

1 John 1:9

In order to restore right relationships, we may need to confess to others as well as to God, for we cannot be right with God and wrong with others.

The sincerity of our confession may need to be evidenced by *restitution*. Apology may need to be made, a quarrel settled, a debt paid, a relationship terminated, if we are to enjoy renewed fellowship with God and people.

Here arises the question of what we should confess and to whom we should confess it.

As all sin is against God, obviously we should confess to Him every sin of which we are conscious, and we should do it without delay, as soon as we realize we have sinned. Some sins are against God alone, but others are against our fellow humans and thus require confession to them.

The scriptural principle involved would seem to be that the confession should be related to the sin. Where the sin is against God alone, the sin needs to be confessed only to God. There may sometimes be therapeutic value in sharing a problem with another trusted friend, but there is no necessity to do so.

Where the sin is against a fellow person, it should be confessed to the one who has been injured by our sin, and need be confessed to no other. Nothing is gained merely by giving someone else, who is not involved, knowledge of your sin.

Where the sin is against a church or group, the sin should be confessed to the church or group in an appropriate manner, probably to the leader, who could decide what action, if any, should be taken.

What about public confession? In some cases that may be called for, but such cases would be rare. Meetings at which there is intimate public confession of personal sins should not be encouraged, as they are often definitely harmful.

On some occasions, however, especially during times of revival and under the pressure of the Holy Spirit, a person can find relief only by confessing specific sins in prayer, and I have seen that several times. But it has always been accompanied with deep humility and brokenness. Anything that savors of exhibitionism or illegitimate interest should be abjured. (EI)

God-Given Time

John 17:4

Our Lord moved through life with a majestic and measured tread, never in a hurry and yet always thronged by demanding crowds, never giving those who sought His help a sense that He had any more important concerns than their particular interests. What was His secret? Knowing that every person's life is in the plan of God, He realized that His life and all the conditions in which it was to be worked out were under the perfect control of His Father.

Time held no power over Him. On several occasions He asserted that His hour had not yet come. There was the consciousness that His Father's plan had been drawn with such meticulous accuracy that every hour fit into the overall purpose of His life. His calendar had been arranged, and His sole concern on earth was to fulfill the work given Him to do in the allotted hours (John 7:6; 12:23, 27; 13:1; 17:1). Nor would He allow His much-loved mother to interfere with this divinely planned timetable (John 2:4). Deep human affection could not be permitted to affect His schedules, or His Father's plan would be marred (John 11:6, 9).

Small wonder then, that at the close of life He could review it with absolute objectivity and speak the self-approving words: "I have finished the work which thou gavest me to do" (John 17:4 KJV); no part of His life was marred by undue haste or imperfectly completed through lack of time. He found sufficient time in the twenty-four hours of the day to do the whole will of God.

The Lord's corrective word to His disciples, "Are there not twelve hours in the day?" (John 11:9 KJV), seems to suggest a quiet, steady confidence in His Father's purpose and a resulting courage even in face of enemies and danger. Interruptions could not disturb His peace because they had already been provided for in the Father's planning, and the wrath of enemies would have to await His "hour." Thus He could pursue His work undisturbed, knowing it would be "finished." There would be time for all that God meant Him to do, though there might not always be "leisure so much as to eat" (Mark 6:31 KJV). (SC)

The Law of Love

Ephesians 5:2

C hrist sets His own love before us as a model. "A new
commandment I give to you, that you love one another,
even as I have loved you, that you also love one another"
(John 13:34 NASB). The law of love goes further than loving
one's neighbors as oneself; it is to love one another as we love
Him. It is love that takes no thought of the cost. That was
the active principle of Christ's life. Paul, too, exhorts
us to "walk in the way of love, just as Christ loved us and gave
himself up for us as a fragrant offering and sacrifice to God"
(Ephesians 5:2).

Personal preferences or dislikes have nothing to do with
love. We are to love people whom we do not even like. "If you
love those who love you, what credit is that to you? Even sinners love those who love them" (Luke 6:32). Although there
may be those I do not like, I can still will to love them. It is the
will and not the emotions that is supreme.

"He who has My commandments and keeps them is the
one who loves Me; and he who loves Me will be loved
by My Father, and I will love him and will disclose Myself
to him" (John 14:21 NASB). Obedience is the test of love, and

it is rewarded by deepening intimacy. Nothing is said here about emotional reactions—only simple obedience. The key question is not, "How do you feel?" but, "Have you obeyed?" Love is expressed through the will. If we are living obediently, we have John 14:21 as our assurance that we love Him and He loves us. One timid Christian said, "I think I love Him because there are things I refrain from doing for no other reason than that He forbids them, while I do other things simply because He desires them." He passes the test. If Christ's will is to us the law of our lives, His smile of approval will be an adequate reward. (EI)

Thankfulness

1 Thessalonians 5:18

Thanksgiving is not difficult when it flows from our recognition of the temporal and spiritual blessings that we consider desirable. But what of the burdens and disciplines and the sufferings and sorrows of life? Surely we cannot be expected to give thanks for those! But this is exactly what God does expect us to do. We are left with no option if we are His obedient children. We must be "always giving thanks to God the Father for everything, in the name of our Lord Jesus Christ" (Ephesians 5:20). These commands are devastatingly inclusive.

No one would suggest that this is always easy, but it is always possible, or God would not expect it of us. There is an Arab proverb that says, "All sunshine makes a desert," and it is true that if life were all joy and prosperity, unmixed with sorrow and adversity, our characters would be immeasurably poorer. Our loving Father knows the exact proportions in which to mix these ingredients, and we should thankfully and without question accept His dealings with us as the very best for us.

The correct response of the heart is expressed in *The Scottish Prayer Book*: "We praise Thee for the grace by which Thou dost enable us so to bear the ills of the present world, that our souls are enriched by a fuller experience of Thy love, a more childlike dependence on Thy will, and a deeper sympathy with the suffering and the sad."

On his way to exile, John Chrysostom exclaimed, "Thank God for everything." Thanking God in one of his matchless letters, Samuel Rutherford wrote, "O, what I owe to the furnace, the file and the hammer of my Lord Jesus!"

A missionary was greatly discouraged. He knew that his work was not progressing as it should. One day, while visiting another missionary, he saw a motto card on the wall: *TRY THANKSGIVING!* It was an arrow to his soul. He suddenly realized that this element had been largely missing from his prayers.

There had been plenty of asking God for things he desired and needed; he had asked desperately at times but had forgotten to thank Him for what he received. He began to count his blessings and to pour out his heart in thanksgiving. (PP)

Humility as a Primary Virtue

Luke 9:48

The works of the great philosophers of past days do not exalt humility as a virtue. Their lives will be examined in vain for evidence of true Christian humility. The reverse is the case. There is no word in either Greek or Latin that expresses the Christian idea of humility. The word *lowly* (KJV; *humble*, NIV), which Jesus appropriated to himself, is employed by ethical philosophers such as Socrates, Plato, and Xenophon in a derogatory sense. Even Josephus, the Hebrew historian and moralist, invested the word with a similar meaning. "Humility is a vice with the heathen moralists," said J. B. Lightfoot.

Not until Jesus came with His peerless life and matchless teaching was humility elevated to the level of a primary virtue. Humility as a grace is a foundation stone of Christianity. Since the Greeks used the word generally as signifying someone base or mean-spirited, it is readily understood that our Lord's pronouncements on the subject introduced His disciples to a startlingly new and revolutionary scale of values. "Those who humble themselves will be exalted" (Matthew 23:12). "It is the one who is least among you all who is the greatest" (Luke 9:48). It was a difficult lesson for them to master, that humility was to be desired, not despised.

Meekness plus lowliness equals humility. Meekness is humility in relation to God. Lowliness is humility in relation to man. It is possible to be meek and not lowly. Jesus was just as meek toward God as He was lowly before man.

In common usage, meekness is almost synonymous with weakness, or an inferiority complex, and is usually attributed to those who are insignificant. Yet our divine Lord crowned this modest character quality as queen of virtues. Otto Borchert contrasts the genuine humility of the Lord, which manifested itself in the utter absence of any striving after magnification or originality, with Muhammad, who was always sensitive to his personal appearance. The vanity of Buddha peeps through the rags of his beggar's cloak. But Jesus moved about in the unaffected guise of ordinary folk, and they were attracted to Him. "He humbled himself" (Philippians 2:8). (31 Days)

Extravagant Service

Mark 14:1–9

"Why this waste of perfume?" (Mark 14:4). Why not do something useful with the money it would bring on the market? Why not be practical? You serve God best by serving His creatures. Think of the number of poor people it would have fed! True, it would have fed many, but thank God it was not sold. These men in the house of Simon were thinking practically but not giving Jesus His proper place.

In His ministry Jesus had demonstrated abundantly that He was not indifferent to the plight of the poor. He was constantly ministering to their physical as well as their spiritual needs. It must have hurt this woman deeply when His disciples so harshly rebuked her.

She had some other options open to her: (1) she could have sold the perfume—and turned it into hard cash and done something "useful" with it; (2) she could have saved it as provision for her old age; (3) she could have used it on herself, to enhance her beauty in the Lord's eyes. Are not somewhat similar options open to us in our relationship to the Lord?

"What a waste!" many said when the brilliant young Cambridge scholar Henry Martyn, who at the age of twenty had gained the highest award in mathematics the world had to offer, threw away his prospects for seven years of missionary work. But in those seven years he gave the world the New Testament in three of the major languages of the East.

"What a waste!" many said when William Borden, heir to the Borden millions, turned his back on his alluring prospects to become a missionary to the Muslims and died before he reached the field. But that proved to be fruitful waste, for his biography, *Borden of Yale*, has influenced thousands toward the mission field.

Perhaps God is not so economical and utilitarian as we are. What waste and "lavish spending" we see in His creation! But there are some things of the heart and the spirit that cannot be measured in cold cash.

How much do we know in practice of this seemingly wasteful and extravagant expenditure of ourselves in His service out of simple love for Him? Or are we stingy and calculating in our self-giving? "Whoever sows sparingly will also reap sparingly" (2 Corinthians 9:6). (SD)

The Meaning of Meekness

Psalm 42:1

The word *meek* is more than an unassuming personality or mere mild disposition. Its meaning has been distorted by the line in the children's hymn "Gentle Jesus, meek and mild." He was meek but was far from mild. The impression the hymn leaves is that Jesus was rather weak and ineffective. In fact, He was the very opposite of weak.

Was it mildness He displayed when, alone and with an uplifted whip, He drove the materialistic traffickers with their sheep and cattle out of the temple? He was anything but servile and spineless. When He asked the disciples who men said that He was, they replied, "Some say Elijah, some John the Baptist"—two of the most rugged characters in the Bible! The word *meek* was used of a horse that had been broken and domesticated, giving the idea of energy and power, controlled and directed.

In heaven, the seven angels sing the song of Moses and the Lamb (Revelation 15:3)—Moses, the meekest man on earth, and Jesus, who said, "I am meek and lowly in heart." But both could blaze with sinless anger when the interests of God were at stake. Meekness is no spineless quality.

This virtue challenges the world's standards. "Stand up for your rights!" is the strident cry of our day. "The world is yours if you can get it." Jesus said, on the contrary, that the world is yours if you renounce it. The meek, not the aggressive, inherit the earth. The meek have an inheritance. The worldly have no future.

"Blessed are those who hunger and thirst for righteousness, for they will be filled" (Matthew 5:6) or "O the bliss of the unsatisfied."

The blessing promised here is not for mere wistfulness or lukewarm desire for God. It is for those who have a passionate craving not after happiness alone but after righteousness—a right relationship with God. The truly blessed person is the one who hungers and thirsts after God himself, not only the blessings He gives. David knew that aspiration when he wrote, "As the deer pants for streams of water, so my soul pants for you, my God" (Psalm 42:1). (SD)

Giving beyond the Limit

2 Corinthians 8:2

"It is more blessed to give than to receive" (Acts 20:35). By divine decree, what I give comes back to me in greater spiritual blessing.

An English nobleman who lay dying said remorsefully,

"What I spent, I had;
What I kept, I lost;
What I *gave* I have."

What did the early church practice in terms of giving to the church and other causes? One might have expected the wealthy, richly gifted Corinthian church to be Paul's model. Instead, it was the poverty-stricken colonial church in Macedonia, rather than in Corinth, that demonstrated and experienced the superior blessedness of generous giving (2 Corinthians 8:1–5).

They were remarkable people. In striking contrast to their deep poverty and affliction shone the riches of their abounding liberality: "That in a great ordeal of affliction their abundance of joy and their deep poverty overflowed in the wealth of their liberality" (v. 2 NASB). Despite their limited resources they did not shrink from giving to the point of costly sacrifice. They calculated the maximum they could give and then went beyond it (v. 3). The question with them was not, "How little?" but, "How much?"

It is a common tendency even among Christians in our day to spend beyond the limit of our means, but have we ever emulated the Macedonians? "For I testify that according to their ability, and beyond their ability they gave of their own accord, begging us with much urging for the favor of participation in the support of the saints" (vv. 3–4 NASB).

What an extraordinary picture! The donor is the one who does the begging! The donor is the one who takes the initiative. Since they gave beyond the limit of their means, they were obviously looking to God to supply their other needs. They gave by principle, not by impulse. Their giving grew out of their surrender to Christ (v. 5).

The Macedonian Christians set us a noble example of liberality, with the result that they themselves experienced "abundance of joy" (v. 2 NASB). (EI)

Faith and Sight

2 Corinthians 5:7

"We walk by faith, not by sight" (2 Corinthians 5:7 KJV). Two principles may govern the Christian's life: the principle of faith and the principle of sight. Sight is caught up in the material and visible; faith is occupied with the spiritual and unseen. Sight is equated with worldly prudence that guides the natural senses; faith is actually heavenly wisdom that guides the enlightened soul. Sight declares that only present things have existence; faith gives existence to future things in the next world.

These two principles are in constant conflict in each of us. There is no such thing as peaceful coexistence between them. They are mutually exclusive because they are absolutely contradictory. In each of us there is a Jacob as well as an Israel, a Simon as well as a Peter, and each ceaselessly strives to gain the victory. Before Jabbok, Jacob lived on the principle of sight; after Jabbok, he lived on that of faith. It was Pentecost that weaned Peter from sight and enabled him to live by faith.

The circumstances of life are designed to give us the opportunity to practice one principle or the other. Jacob and

Esau were surrounded by the same conditions and influences, but there was a different outcome. Esau fell, but Jacob eventually stood. Jacob walked by faith, and Esau chose the path of sight, of worldly prudence.

Faith, like eyesight, has no abstract existence. It does not exist apart from the object on which it is directed. Nor is it a mere subjective state of mind. There is always an actual fact corresponding to it that gives faith substance. It is not a future hope but a present fact. Hope is expecting, faith is receiving and accepting.

Faith always involves a risk, but sight is too hesitant to take a step into the seeming void. "What if?" is not in faith's vocabulary. Faith is not faith unless we act upon it, for faith is active, not passive. On which principle are we conducting our lives? (CC)

The Supremacy of Love

1 Corinthians 12:31; 13:2

"And I show you a still more excellent way ... If I ... do not have love, I am nothing" (1 Corinthians 12:31; 13:2 NASB). Sin may be defined as missing the mark, transgressing the law of God, or lack of conformity to the moral law of God. But in 1 Corinthians 13, the great classic chapter on love, we are presented with another conception. The standard of what we ought to be is not the Ten Commandments but the perfect character of Christ, who was the image of the invisible God. Sin includes anything in which we fail to conform to the perfection of Christ and especially failure to love God and our neighbor.

In his letter, Paul deals with failure and sin in the Corinthian church, and this wonderful chapter is one of the instruments he uses. "The beautiful lyric is thus the lancet," said James Moffatt. And a lancet is used for probing a sore and allowing the offensive pus to drain away. Each quality of love mentioned here is the perfect answer to some infection of sin in the Corinthian church—and in us too. For example, envy is the fault of those who feel inferior, and boasting the fault of those who consider themselves superior. Love is the answer to both sins—and to every other sin too.

In the dazzling light of this love, unworthy motivation is exposed, hypocrisy unmasked, and insincerity unveiled. The chapter forms a beautiful portrait of the life of Christ. Substitute *Christ* for *love* in verses 4–8 and note how perfectly every quality of love is matched in His matchless character. But try the experiment of substituting *I* for *love*. Can you not feel the sharp stab of the lancet? Paul contrasts love with the charismatic gifts so prized by the brilliant Corinthians and shows that they are no acceptable substitute.

If we have the courage to use this lyric on our lives as a lancet, we may find it a devastating experience, for it will probe many hidden "infections" in our lives. But the lancet is used only as a probe to a cure. What is the cure? Read verses 4–8, and substitute *Christ in me* for *love*. And Christ *is* in me. (CC)

Time and Eternity

Ephesians 5:16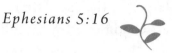

I s time found in the ticking of the clock or the moving of a shadow? Calendars and clocks are only mechanical means by which we record our consciousness of time, not time itself. As we commonly use the word, it means "duration" or "a stretch of duration in which things happen." But perhaps the most helpful definition of time is "duration turned to account." Dr. John R. Mott viewed time as our lives measured out for work, the measure of the capacity of our lives to complete His tasks.

Paul counseled the Ephesian believers to "redeem the time," or as Weymouth renders it, "buy up the opportunities," for time is opportunity. Note that time becomes ours by purchase—it has to be redeemed, or bought. We exchange it for certain occupations and activities, important or otherwise, and this is where the importance of a planned life comes in. When we say we don't have time, it may only be that we do not know how to make use of the opportunity time affords us. Time is a God-given stewardship for which we must render account, and our use of it will determine the value of our contribution to our day and generation.

The difference between one person and another is found largely in the use of time. "All attainments and achievements are conditioned by the full use of time," wrote a master of that art. "If we progress in the economy of time, we are learning to live. If we fail here, we fail everywhere. No man is or does more than his time allows him to do." In his *Holy Living*, Jeremy Taylor wrote: "God hath given to man a short time here upon earth and yet upon this short time eternity depends. No man is a better merchant than he that lays out his time upon God."

The solemn thing about time is, of course, that it can be lost, and time lost can never be regained. It cannot be hoarded; it must be spent. It cannot be postponed; it is irretrievably lost. How supremely important, then, that we make full use of the time allotted to us for the fulfillment of our life purpose! (SC)

Love Is Patient and Kind

1 Corinthians 13:4

"Love suffereth long." It is significant that the patience of love comes first. It is not so much what love can do as how long love can be sustained without breaking down, for it is our long-suffering with others that is addressed in this passage. Love's severest tests come in the realm of our relations with others. "Lord, how oft shall my brother sin against me and I forgive him? till seven times?" Peter doubtless thought he was being very generous until he heard the Master's reply: "I say not unto thee, Until seven times: but, Until seventy times seven" (Matthew 18:21–22 KJV).

Love does not balk at the first hurdle but finishes the race. No matter how strong the provocation, love is never betrayed by ill-advised speech or hasty action that will later be bitterly regretted. Love knows how to hold its peace even amid gross injustice. Love's long-suffering found its crowning demonstration on the slopes of Mount Calvary, where the supreme sufferer, instead of calling down curses, prayed for His tormentors.

"Love is kind." Kindness has been defined as a way to place oneself at the disposal of others, regardless of their position or attitude. What a benediction kind people are in a cold and unsympathetic world. They are always on the lookout to be of service to someone else.

Lady Bartle Frere once requested a young guest to meet her husband at the railway station.

"But how shall I recognize him?" asked the young man. "I have never met him."

"Just look for a tall gentleman helping someone," was the response. "That will be my husband." (SP)

The Greatest Is Love

Galatians 5:6

L et us speak the truth by all means, but let it be in love.

The power to unravel "all mysteries," the possessions of profound erudition, the ability to plumb and propound the deep things of God—all these count for nothing in the absence of love. As Matthew Henry put it, "A clear and deep head is of no significance without a benevolent and loving heart." Love is more than knowledge.

Love triumphs over miracle-working faith. No believer should minimize the value and importance of faith in every aspect of the Christian life, and Paul certainly did not. The vital part it plays cannot be overestimated, for "without faith it is impossible to please God" (Hebrews 11:6). But it should always be remembered that "faith worketh by love" (Galatians 5:6 KJV). If faith is out of proportion to love, her apparent success is really failure. Even the receiving of spectacular answers to prayer is no acceptable substitute for a love-filled life. We have often prayed, "Lord, increase our faith," but someone has suggested the addition of another petition: "Lord, increase our love, lest our faith be in vain." Love is more than faith.

The superlative excellence of faith over heartless charity is emphasized. Few activities secure our approval more than philanthropy, and rightly so. Yet, "if I share out all my goods morsel by morsel, but have not love, it profiteth me nothing," says Deissman. The purity of the motive determines the quality of the action. Ananias emulated Barnabas in making a magnificent gift, but his unworthy motive robbed the act of all spiritual value and rendered the gift wholly unacceptable to God. We should closely scrutinize the motive that prompts our philanthropy lest love of attention or desire for approval displace true love of others. Love is more than philanthropy. (SP)

The Potter and the Clay

Jeremiah 18:5-6

The patriot-prophet Jeremiah was heartbroken. Despite his tears and entreaties, his beloved nation had proven stubborn and was drifting further and further from God. His earnest endeavors to avert catastrophe had proved fruitless. He had exhausted all his own resources, and there seemed no alternative to deserved judgment.

It was just when he had reached this crisis that God gave Jeremiah a vision of hope. "Go down to the potter's house" the Lord said, "and there I will give you my message" (Jeremiah 18:2). Although Israel had persistently thwarted the divine purpose of blessing, if the nation would repent and once again yield to His touch, the heavenly Potter would make it into a new nation and give it another chance, even at this late hour.

Although the vision was a contemporary message to Israel, the application is timeless. Just as the elements of the potter's art are essentially the same as in Jeremiah's day, so are God's methods and dealings with His children in every age. The context and trappings may differ, but the underlying principles are unchanging.

When Jeremiah went obediently to the potter's house, he saw the revolving wheel controlled by the potter's foot; a pile of clay inert and unable to improve its condition, of no intrinsic value; a pot of water for use in softening the clay and making it moldable; a scrap heap on which the potter cast the pots that had failed to realize his design; and, of course, he saw the skillful and experienced potter himself. "Then the word of the LORD came to me," Jeremiah wrote. "'Can I not do with you, Israel, as this potter does?' declares the LORD. 'Like clay in the hand of the potter, so are you in my hand'" (vv. 5–6).

That assertion of the absolute, sovereign power of God sounds rather harsh and forbidding. His power is so final, and we are so powerless. But Isaiah the prophet softens the picture: "Yet you, LORD, are our Father. We are the clay, you are the potter; we are all the work of your hand" (Isaiah 64:8).

True, God is sovereign in His power, but He also has a father's heart. We can be absolutely certain that His sovereignty will never clash with His paternity. All His dealings with His frail and failing children are dictated by unchanging love. (SD)

Reaping the Consequences

2 Peter 2:15

B alak had heard of the fame of the prophet Balaam, so in superstitious fear he summoned him to put a curse on the Israelites and thus secure their defeat. Of course there would be an adequate reward for Balak if he succeeded.

If he were a true prophet of Jehovah, Balaam should have dismissed the proposition out of hand and sent the delegation packing back to the king. God's command was so clear and unequivocal that there were no grounds for postponing giving them a final answer. "You must not put a curse on those people, because they are blessed" (Numbers 22:12) were God's words.

But Balaam toyed with temptation, for he "loved the wages of wickedness" (2 Peter 2:15). So he left the door open for a further approach from Balak. Parleying with temptation is always fraught with danger. The serpent should be killed, not stroked.

Balak, refusing to take no for an answer, dispatched an even more prestigious delegation and promised an even more generous reward. Balaam tried to persuade the Lord to change His mind and allow him to go to Balak. When God saw that he had determined to secure the reward, whatever the cost, He went to him in the night and said, "Since these men have come to summon you, go with them, but do only what I tell you" (Numbers 22:20). It was when Balaam was on his way with the princes to King Balak that the mysterious incident of the talking donkey was enacted.

Had God changed His mind? Not for a moment. Since Balaam refused to take no for an answer, God said in effect, "If I cannot keep you from disobeying me, go, and reap the consequences." There is a limit to the divine patience with one who tries to get the best of both worlds. (EL)

Paul's Thorn

2 Corinthians 12:7

"Lest I should be exalted above measure . . . there was given to me a thorn in the flesh, the messenger of Satan to buffet me" (2 Corinthians 12:7 KJV). In this brief biographical glimpse, Paul shares one of his deepest spiritual experiences. For this we can thank the opponents in the Corinthian church, who challenged his apostleship and compelled him to defend himself (v. 11). Robert Louis Stevenson, though a very sick man, wrote: "I should think myself a trifler and in very bad taste if I introduced the world to these unimportant privacies." Paul exercised a similar restraint, and it was only the necessity of vindicating his authority that compelled him to share a deep spiritual experience.

Paul tells of being "caught up to paradise," the realm where God is fully manifested and where he heard "things that no one is permitted to tell" (v. 4). But such an ecstatic experience included its own dangers for him, dangers with which God had His own method of dealing with Paul. He was in peril of succumbing to spiritual pride, which is clear from his own statement. Few things tend to inflate people with a sense of their own importance more than the possession of great gifts of intellect or the enjoyment of unusual experiences; and nothing more surely disqualifies them in God's service. So God brought into Paul's life an equalizing factor, so that his ministry would not be limited. "There was given to me a thorn."

We should be grateful to Paul for his reluctance concerning the nature of this thorn, which is not the main point of his disclosure. Instead, he concentrates on the unchanging principles involved. His was a representative case from which believers of all time could draw strength. *Thorn* conveys the idea of a painful stake on which he was impaled. It was something deflating in its effect, and something Satan could exploit. Satan intended it for ill, but God meant it for good.

Our thorn may be some physical disability, some temperamental weakness, some family sorrow; but whatever it is, instead of being a limiting handicap it can be a heavenly advantage. Despite Paul's thrice-repeated prayer, God did not remove the thorn. Instead, He promised compensating grace, "My grace is sufficient for thee" (v. 9 KJV). Paul accepted this grace, and his strength was made perfect in weakness. (CC)

The Passover Song

Psalm 118:29

At the feasts of Passover, Pentecost, Dedication, and Tabernacles, part of the ritual was the singing of Psalms 113–118, which were originally one song. Together, those psalms were known as the *Hallel*, a term meaning "to praise." It was the practice to divide the group of hymns into two parts, one of which was repeated in the middle of the banquet, the other reserved until the end.

Jesus found the joy of doing His Father's will so utterly satisfying that, with clear knowledge of what lay ahead, He was able to sing with insight, "This is the day which the LORD has made; [I will] rejoice and be glad in it" (Psalm 118:24 NASB). Although He knew that in a few hours His Father's face would be averted from Him because of His identification with the sin of the world, He still sang, "Give thanks to the LORD, for he is good; his love endures forever" (Psalm 118:29).

Not many days before, a remarkable demonstration had taken place when Jesus entered Jerusalem sitting on a donkey. "A very large crowd spread their cloaks on the road, while others cut branches from the trees and spread them on the road. The crowds that went ahead of him and those that followed shouted, 'Hosanna to the Son of David! Blessed is he who comes in the name of the Lord! Hosanna in the highest heaven!' When Jesus entered Jerusalem, the whole city was stirred and asked, 'Who is this?' The crowds answered, 'This is Jesus, the prophet from Nazareth in Galilee'" (Matthew 21:8–11).

As He sang these words, He was anticipating that in a few hours the adulation of the crowd would turn into the sullen roar "Crucify Him!" Even that did not quench His song.

Not only did He go to the cross with a song on His lips, but the last words of the song were words of thanksgiving: "Give thanks to the LORD, for he is good; his love endures forever" (Psalm 118:29). With these words, amid the shadows cast by the Passover moon, He led the little band to the olive garden.

What can we learn from the Passover song? We learn that we can turn our trouble into treasure and our sorrow into song. We can sing the song of faith in the darkest hour. Sorrow and singing are not incompatible. (31 Days)

Christh in Paul

Colossians 3:4

Paul's personality was not obliterated because Christ lived inside him. "I live," he said, "yet not I, but Christ liveth in me" (Galatians 2:20 KJV). He did not become any the less Paul because he was indwelt by Christ. Indeed, he became more and more the Paul God intended him to be; the ideal Paul who was a chosen vessel to the Lord. We need not fear the fullest surrender to Christ, for He enhances and dignifies our personalities. He imparts holy qualities that are absent and brings to the surface powers in our personalities that were latent. Paul became a different Paul, but a greater and a better Paul. Apart from the indwelling and control by the Spirit of Christ, the world would probably have heard little of him. Instead, his influence has been one of the dominating features of the last two millennia.

Christ lived in Paul in the sense that from within the core of his yielded personality Christ reproduced His own gracious and radiant life. Through Paul's letters, characteristic of him and bearing all the marks of his personality, Christ was able to convey His message to successive generations of Christians.

Through constant communion with Christ, Paul became less and less like the Saul of his persecuting days and more and more like the Christ with whom he had companionship. He lived a life that emanated from the same source, was inspired by the same ideals, governed by the same standards, and enabled by the same power as his indwelling Lord. His life indeed was grounded in someone else. (CC)

The Judge Is Judged

John 19:7

Pilate endeavored to get the Jews to consent to Jesus's release since none of the charges against Him had been substantiated, but all to no avail. They would be appeased by nothing less than the shedding of blood. Barabbas the murderer was preferred to Jesus the sinless Son of God in terms of freedom. Jesus was declared innocent, He was scourged, clothed in purple, and crowned with thorns. Only at the end did the true charge come to the surface. "The Jewish leaders insisted, 'We have a law, and according to that law he must die, because he claimed to be the Son of God'" (John 19:7).

At last the cowardly Pilate succumbed to their threats and delivered Him up to be crucified. Then he washed his hands, according to the Jewish custom, saying: "I am innocent of this man's blood" (Matthew 27:24). "His blood is on us and on our children" was their fateful response (v. 25). As Maclaren points out, he took his revenge by placing upon the cross the announcement that was so galling to them, "The king of the Jews."

On what legal grounds was Jesus condemned? None! He was tried six times and acquitted three times, and yet was condemned to die. The Light of the World had shone with such a searching beam that a guilty world had to try to extinguish it.

What is the importance of the trial? "It lies in the fact," says W. Robertson Nicoll, "that the issue raised was Christ's claim to be the Son of God, the Messiah of Israel, and a King. He was tried unfairly and judged unjustly, but the true issue was raised. He died, then, because before the Jews He claimed to be the Son of God and the Messiah, and before Pilate to be Christ and King."

All generations since have felt that the judged was the Judge. The men were really standing before the judgment seat of Christ, and they all appeared with their many failings as contrasted with the Light of the World. (31 Days)

Prayer and Conscience

1 John 3:21–22

Instead of having confidence in approaching God, we may be held back by a condemning heart. John the apostle assured those to whom he was writing that whatever condemns us in our conscience hinders prayer. Until known sin is judged and renounced, we pray and plead in vain. "Beloved, if our heart does not condemn us, we have confidence before God; and whatever we ask we receive from Him" (1 John 3:21–22 NASB).

If we know of some reason our conscience condemns us, it is for us to deal with it and do all in our power to put it right with God and people. Until we do, we will endeavor in vain to pray the prayer of faith. More often than not this is why we are unable to exercise appropriating faith when we pray.

What are we to do if some subtle sense of guilt and condemnation descends on our spirits? We examine our hearts but can assign no reason for the distress. It is a nameless depression of spirit, a vague disturbance that prevents the soul from rising to God in the prayer of faith. How is this condition to be remedied?

First, let us sincerely ask God to reveal to us if there is some real but unrecognized sin that lies at the root of this sense of condemnation. If He reveals something to us, let us put it right at the first opportunity. Confidence toward God will thus be restored, and our prayers will receive their answers.

But should there be no such revelation of sin, we are justified in concluding that the obscuring cloud originates in enemy territory. Many have found it helpful to pray in such circumstances, "Lord, if this sense of condemnation comes from Your Spirit's conviction, make my sin clear to me, and I shall confess and put it right. But if it comes from Satan, then on the grounds of Calvary's victory, I refuse and reject it."

This attitude of acceptance of the divine dealing but rejection of the satanic intrusion has often brought deliverance and renewed freedom in prayer, for it is true that "if our heart does not condemn us, we have confidence before God." (PP)

Ways to Worship

John 5:39

How can I get to know better and more intimately the Christ who reveals the Father? I can know Him primarily through the Scriptures as they are illuminated by the inspiring Holy Spirit. They are rich with material to feed and stimulate worship and adoration. The Scriptures are the only tangible way of knowing Him, as Jesus himself indicated: "You search the Scriptures because you think that in them you have eternal life; it is these that testify about Me" (John 5:39 NASB).

In the Bible, we have the full and adequate revelation of the vast scope of the divine nature. Great tracts of truth await our exploration. Great themes—God's sovereignty, truth, holiness, wisdom, love, faithfulness, patience, mercy—illumined and made relevant to us by the Holy Spirit, will feed the flame of our worship.

The devotional use of a good hymnbook, especially the sections that deal with the person and work of the members of the Trinity, will prove a great aid to a deeper, more intimate knowledge of God. Not all of us find it easy to express our deepest feelings or to utter our love to God. When we are in the place of prayer, we are painfully conscious of the poor quality of our thoughts of God and the inadequacy of words to express those thoughts. God has given the church gifted hymn writers to help His less gifted children pour out their worship and praise, and we can take their words and make them our own. Many of the church's great hymns are the nearest thing to divine inspiration.

We should, however, beware of conceiving of worship as being confined solely to the realm of thought, for in Scripture it is also linked with service. "You shall worship the Lord your God, and serve Him only," were our Lord's words to Satan (Matthew 4:10 NASB). We should not separate what God has joined, in terms of worship and service. Worship is no substitute for service, nor is service a substitute for worship. But true worship must always be expressed in loving service. (EI)

Unanswered Prayer

Matthew 17:20

Our Lord's brother gives one reason for unanswered prayer: "When you ask, you do not receive, because you ask with wrong motives" (James 4:3). God does not attempt to answer every self-centered petition, but He does promise to answer every prayer that is according to His good and perfect will.

It may be that our prayer was not the prayer of faith but only the prayer of hope. Jesus said, "According to your faith let it be done to you" (Matthew 9:29), not according to your hope. Are many of your prayers only prayers of hope?

Or we may have been substituting faith in prayer for faith in God. We are not told anywhere to have faith in prayer but to "have faith in God," the One who answers the prayer. This is more than a matter of semantics. Sometimes we sigh, "Our prayers are so weak and ineffective!" or "My faith is so small!" Jesus anticipated this reaction when He said, "Truly I tell you, if you have faith as small as a mustard seed, you can say to this mountain, 'Move from here to there' and it will move. Nothing will be impossible for you" (Matthew 17:20).

The naked eye sees little difference between a grain of sand and a mustard seed, but there is a world of difference between the two. In the mustard seed is the germ of life. It is not the size of our faith that is important, but whether it is a living faith in a living God.

Mature disciples will not become discouraged because of a delay in the answer to their prayer. They know that a delayed answer is not necessarily a denied answer.

God's timing is infallible. He takes every factor and contingency into account. We often want to pluck unripe fruit, but He will not be pressured into premature action.

If He in His wisdom delays the answer to our prayer, that delay will in the long run prove to be for our good. (See Hebrews 12:10.) It will be either because He has some better thing for us or because there is something He desires to achieve in our lives that can come about in no other way. (SD)

Interceding for the Lost

Colossians 4:12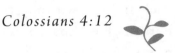

The worker whose supreme desire and passion is to be used in cooperation with the Holy Spirit in the winning of converts to Christ must master in some degree the holy art of intercession. If the Master wept and prayed over lost souls, then His servant must do the same. Prayer must always occupy a preeminent place in an evangelism program, for the salvation of the soul is not a human but a divine work. Only through prayer can the power of God be released.

If prayer, then, occupies so important a place, it follows that whatever hinders us in its exercise must be sacrificed. Any price is worth paying that will make us more powerful in prayer. If God is to answer our prayers, we must be sure that we are standing on praying ground. The psalmist warns: "If I regard [cling to] iniquity in my heart, the Lord will not hear me" (Psalm 66:18 KJV), let alone answer me. Before we are on true holy ground, we must have renounced every sin about which the Holy Spirit has convicted us. Have you done this, or is there a barrier between your soul and God? You will know when the last thing has been dealt with.

Then it is necessary that we have a heart separated from itself and its own concerns, a heart that is able to bear the burden of lost souls and to intercede for them in the birth process until the new life is implanted. Listen to the apostle Paul as he prays, and note how his prayers are all for others. "I could wish that myself were accursed from Christ for my brethren, my kinsmen according to the flesh" (Romans 9:3 KJV). Mark Epaphras, "always labouring fervently . . . in prayers" (Colossians 4:12 KJV). (DA)

Supernatural Resources

Ephesians 6:18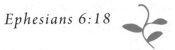

"Give yourselves wholly to prayer and entreaty; pray on every occasion in the power of the Spirit" (Ephesians 6:18 NEB). Prayer demands more than mere human power and energy for its supernatural task, and the Holy Spirit supplies it. He is the Spirit of power as well as the Spirit of prayer. Mere human energy of heart, mind, and will can achieve only human results. But praying in the power of the Spirit releases supernatural resources.

It is the Spirit's delight to aid us in our physical and moral weakness in our prayer life, for the praying heart labors under three limiting handicaps; but in each of them we can count on the Spirit's assistance. Sometimes we are kept from prayer because of the conscious sin of our hearts. The Spirit will lead and enable us to appropriate the cleansing of the blood of Christ, which will silence the accusations of the adversary and remove the sense of guilt and pollution. We are always hampered by the limiting ignorance of our minds.

The Spirit who knows the mind of God will share that knowledge with us as we wait on Him. Then we will have the quiet, clear conviction that our request is in the will of God, and faith will be kindled. We are often earthbound through the numbing infirmities and limitations of our bodies. The Spirit will quicken our mortal bodies in response to our faith and enable us to rise above physical and environmental conditions.

Are we receiving His help along these lines? Is this our present experience? Have we slipped into an independence of the Spirit? Are we habitually praying in the Spirit and receiving full answers to the strategic prayers He inspires? Our intellectual appreciation of spiritual truths often outruns our practical experience of their implications and benefits. (BB)

The Model Prayer

Matthew 6:9–13 (KJV)

The true spirit in which prayer is to be offered to God is exemplified in the Lord's Prayer. We are to pray in an unselfish spirit. It is "Our Father," not "My Father." Ours is to be a childlike spirit, the approach of a son or daughter to a father. The prayer is to be offered in a reverent spirit: "Hallowed be thy name"; in a loyal spirit: "Thy kingdom come"; in a submissive spirit: "Thy will be done in earth"; in a dependent spirit: "Give us this day our daily bread"; in a repentant spirit: "Forgive us our debts"; in a forgiving spirit: "As we forgive our debtors"; in a humble spirit: "Lead us not into temptation but deliver us from evil"; in a triumphant spirit: "Thine is the kingdom, and the power"; in a hopeful spirit: "[Thine is] the glory, for ever."

The prayer embraces every relationship. Child and father: "Our Father"; worshiper and God: "Hallowed be thy name"; subject and king: "Thy kingdom come"; servant and master: "Thy will be done"; beggar and benefactor: "Give us"; pilgrim and guide: "Lead us."

There is a beautiful symmetry in its structure. It starts with an invocation and concludes with a doxology; between these are six petitions. The first three are directed godward and for His glory; the last three are human-directed and concern our need.

There is a missionary slant to the prayer. As we use it in our quiet time, we will ask that His name may be hallowed throughout the whole world. We will pray that His kingdom will know no frontiers. We will petition that His will may be done throughout the whole earth.

This is the model of the way in which we are to pray, rather than the exact form we are to use. It is capable of endless expansion. Is anything excluded from it that would add to God's glory or would more completely meet a person's need? As we pray in this way we have the glorious assurance that our Father who sees in secret will reward us openly. (BB)

Prayer and the Will of God

Philippians 2:13

How can we know with certainty what is, and what is not, the will of God? If I do not know with certainty that my petition is in the will of God, how can I pray in faith? There must be a reasonable and satisfying answer, or God could be charged with unfairness in imposing a condition we are unable to fulfill.

It is my conviction that the answer to our questions will gradually emerge as we engage in the practice of prayer rather than while we are studying its theory. Study is, of course, necessary, but it must not be divorced from actual praying.

True prayer is not asking God for what we want, but for what *He* wants. This is implicit in the petition of the pattern prayer: "Thy will be done in earth" (Matthew 6:10 KJV); and as William Barclay remarks, it is not "Thy will be changed," but "Thy will be done." Prayer is not a convenient method of getting one's own way or of bending God to one's desires.

Prayer is the means by which our desires can be redirected and aligned with the will of God. As we expectantly pray for light concerning the will of God on any matter, if our desires are not in line with His will, He will make it clear.

If we are willing, He will change and redirect our desires, as Paul assures us: "It is God who is at work in you, both to will and to work for His good pleasure" (Philippians 2:13 NASB).

We must not imagine that God will indiscriminately grant anything we desire. What would happen in the world if this were the case? What chaos! The farmer prays urgently for rain to save his crops on the same day that the vacationer earnestly prays for sunshine. People in Britain pray in time of war for the success of their armies, while the Germans are praying for victory for their troops. God cannot grant both requests.

How are we to pray in such situations? Only one prayer is appropriate: "Lord, we do not know what to pray for as we ought; may thy will be done on earth in this matter as it is done in heaven" (see Romans 8:26 and Matthew 6:10). (PP)

Comfort to Comfort Others

2 Corinthians 1:3–4

"Blessed be the God and Father of our Lord Jesus Christ, the Father of mercies and God of all comfort, who comforts us in all our affliction so that we will be able to comfort those who are in any affliction with the comfort with which we ourselves are comforted by God" (2 Corinthians 1:3–4 NASB). One of the great preachers of the twentieth century, sensitive to the needs of his generation, declared that if he could live his life over again, he would devote more time to the ministry of comfort and encouragement. His assessment of a preacher's role still applies today.

Isaiah described the mission of the Messiah as ministering to the poor, the brokenhearted, the captives, and the blind. God is deeply concerned for His burdened and suffering children. As the "God of all comfort," He comforts them in their sorrows, but with a definite end in view: that their experience of His comfort might equip them to comfort others. Are we using God's comfort ultimately to benefit others, or do we selfishly keep it to ourselves?

The English word *comfort*, used ten times in five verses, is an inadequate translation of the word in Greek. This comfort is more than soothing sympathy; it is comfort that brings strength and courage, a courage that enables us to meet and triumph over the worst that life can bring to us. Interestingly, the word has a derivation similar to *Paraclete*, one of the names of the Holy Spirit, who imparts God's comfort to us.

The personal experience of God's comfort qualifies us to comfort others. If we ourselves experience little trouble and affliction, we won't have a valid ministry of comfort and encouragement to others. God's comfort was one of the main sources of grace that enabled Paul to make the astounding claim that he rejoiced in tribulation. It is one of the consolations of gray hair that, having experienced God's comfort in our times of sorrow and trials of all kinds, we are able to use our experience to bring similar comfort to others. Are we really treating our experience as an investment in the lives of others? If we do, our own burdens will be lightened by sharing how God has comforted us in the past.

"It is possible to escape a multitude of troubles," said J. H. Jowett, "by living an insignificant life. The range of our possible suffering is determined by the largeness and nobility of our aims." Let us covet this ministry of comfort and encouragement. (CC)

PART 3

LORD
OF OUR
FUTURE

Acceptable Worship

Colossians 2:9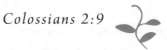

No worship is acceptable to God that ignores or excludes Christ. It is through Christ alone that we have access to the Father (see Ephesians 2:18). "No man cometh unto the Father, but by me," claimed Jesus (John 14:6 KJV). To worship Christ is to worship God, who has revealed himself in Christ. "He that hath seen me hath seen the Father" (v. 9 KJV).

How can we really come to know the Christ who alone reveals God? The answer is, of course, in the Bible, the only tangible means of divine knowledge. "Search the scriptures," said Jesus, "they are they which testify of me" (John 5:39 KJV). In them is the complete and satisfying revelation and interpretation of Jesus Christ. Failure both in worship and in other aspects of prayer is directly traceable to our misuse or ignorance of the Word of God.

The Scriptures are rich in material to stimulate and feed worship. Vast tracts of truth await our exploration and exploitation. God's sovereignty, holiness, love, mercy, patience, faithfulness, wisdom, and grace are evidenced in every book. It is for us to make intelligent use of this divinely inspired prayer book. It is essential that we have a true conception of Christ, lest we be found worshiping a god of our own imagining.

Let it not be thought that worship consists primarily in pleasing emotions and lofty thoughts. It is inseparably united with service. Those who worship their God most devoutly will serve Him most sacrificially. Note the conjunction of the two ideas: "Thou shalt *worship* the Lord thy God, and him only shalt thou *serve*" (Matthew 4:10 KJV, emphasis added). We must not disconnect what God has joined. Worship is no substitute for service, and service is no substitute for worship. True worship on Sunday will express itself in sacrificial service on Monday. To worship is to serve. The blessedness of worship will not stop at service; it will produce transformed character. Inevitably we become increasingly like the blessed One whom we worship. (SP)

Sharing God's Glory

Luke 22:28–30

There are three groups of people who in Scripture are said to share the glory of the enthroned Christ.

The first group includes those who had remained loyal to Christ amid the trials of this earthly life. Their service had not been perfect, but they had remained true despite opposition. "You are those who have stood by me in my trials. And I confer on you a kingdom, just as my Father conferred one on me, so that you may eat and drink at my table in my kingdom and sit on thrones, judging the twelve tribes of Israel" (Luke 22:28–30).

As recognition of their loyalty, they are accorded seats of honor at the heavenly banquet, sitting at His table. If we display a similar loyalty, we shall doubtless receive the same reward.

They will also "sit on thrones, judging the twelve tribes of Israel" (v. 30). In those days, as today, the king as supreme judge of the high court had legal assessors who sat with him, and no doubt this was the figure the Lord had in mind.

The second class of believers who reign with the Lord certainly includes the martyrs for Christ and may possibly include all believers. "Do you not know that the Lord's people will judge the world? And if you are to judge the world, are you not competent to judge trivial cases?" (1 Corinthians 6:2). "I saw thrones on which were seated those who had been given authority to judge. And I saw the souls of those who had been beheaded because of their testimony about Jesus and because of the word of God" (Revelation 20:4).

The third group includes those who are the overcomers among the churches. "To the one who is victorious, I will give the right to sit with me on my throne, just as I was victorious and sat down with my Father on his throne" (Revelation 3:21). "To the one who is victorious and does my will to the end, I will give authority over the nations" (Revelation 2:26). (HB)

The Lamb's Book of Life

Revelation 20:11–12

What does it mean to have one's name written in the Lamb's Book of Life?

Concerning the judgment in front of the great white throne we read, "Then I saw a great white throne...And I saw the dead, great and small, standing before the throne, and books were opened. Another book was opened, which is the book of life. The dead were judged according to what they had done as recorded in the books" (Revelation 20:11–12).

One set of books, then, contains the record of each person's life history. The other book is the Lamb's Book of Life. The first record can bring only condemnation, for all have fallen short of God's standards. In the Book of Life are recorded the names of those who have repented of their sins and exercised saving faith in Christ as Redeemer and Savior.

John Bunyan, in his *Pilgrim's Progress*, describes the armed man who came up to the table where the man with the book and the inkhorn was seated and said, "Set down my name." It is open to anyone to do just that. A living faith in Christ, the Lamb of God who "takes away the sin of the world," is the sole condition for having our names written in that book, and that constitutes our passport through the pearly gates. "They that trust in Jesus Christ," writes Alexander Maclaren, "shall have their names written in the Book of Life; graven on the High Priest's breastplate, and inscribed on His mighty hand and His faithful heart."

Why not make absolutely certain of heaven by opening your heart to Christ the Savior and Lord right now, inviting Him to enter, to cleanse it from sin, and to make it His permanent dwelling place? (HB)

Rewards in Heaven

Luke 18:29

"The whole subject of rewards for the believer in heaven is one that is rarely thought of by the ordinary Christian, or even by the student of the Scriptures. It is at once both a joyous and a solemn theme, and should serve as a potent incentive for holiness of life." So wrote Wilbur M. Smith many years ago, and circumstances have changed little since then with regard to this topic.

There are spiritual teachers who regard the whole concept of rewards for service as a very second-rate motivation. They liken it to bribing a child with candy for good behavior. But Jesus in no way offered support to this viewpoint. The apostle Paul also teaches about rewards in several of his letters.

It goes without saying that no acts of merit of ours can win salvation, for that is a result of God's incredible and unmerited love. But the very fact that Jesus spoke of rewards for service on a number of occasions would indicate that He considered their granting an important article of faith. But in no way did He suggest or imply that service was a method of accumulating merit and thereby receiving salvation. Eternal life is a gift, not a reward.

The language in which the concept of rewards is clothed is highly symbolic and should be interpreted accordingly. Of course, faithful service brings rewards in this life as well as in the life to come. Both are mentioned in the following verse: "'Truly I tell you,' Jesus said to them, 'no one who has left home or wife or brothers or sisters or parents or children for the sake of the kingdom of God will fail to receive many times as much in this age, and in the age to come eternal life'" (Luke 18:29–30). (HB)

Pleading the Promises

Ephesians 3:8

"Every promise of Scripture is a writing of God," said Charles Haddon Spurgeon, "which may be pleaded before Him with this reasonable request, 'Do as Thou hast said.' The Creator will not cheat the creature who depends upon His truth; and far more, the heavenly Father will not break His word to His own child."

What is a promise? A promise is a written or verbal declaration that binds the person who makes it to perform a specified act. When applied to God, it is His pledge to do or refrain from doing a certain thing. Such promises form the basis of the prayer of faith. It is through prayer that these promises are turned into the facts and factors of one's Christian experience.

The validity and dependability of a promise rest on the character and resources of the one who makes it, just as the validity of a bank check depends on the integrity and bank balance of the one who signs it. The holy character and faithfulness of God make His promises credible. "He who promised is faithful," testified the writer of the letter to the

Hebrews (10:23). "Not one word has failed of all His good promise," said the kneeling Solomon (1 Kings 8:56 NASB).

God's promises are thus bound up with His character and rest on four of His divine attributes: (1) His truth, which makes lying impossible; (2) His omniscience, which makes His being deceived or mistaken impossible; (3) His power, which makes everything possible; and (4) His unchangeableness, which precludes wavering or change.

So when we come to God armed with one of His promises, we can do so with the utmost confidence. We can share Abraham's unwavering trust. "With respect to the promise of God, he did not waver in unbelief, but grew strong in faith, giving glory to God, and being fully assured that what God had promised, He was able also to perform" (Romans 4:20–21 NASB). (PP)

The Time of His Coming

Luke 21:31

The Bible tells us a sufficient amount to satisfy our faith, although not always enough to gratify our curiosity. The New Testament was not written to satisfy the inquisitive mind but to glorify the One who is coming again and to stimulate faith in Him. Although we may not know the exact day or hour, the Lord indicated that we could know when His coming was at hand. The coincidence of certain signs would be its sure precursor.

There would be a spiritual sign—widespread apostasy and departure from the faith (2 Thessalonians 2:3; 1 Timothy 4:1). Scoffers would ridicule the idea of His coming (2 Peter 3:3).

There would be political signs, days of peril nationally and socially (2 Timothy 3:1). "Nations will be in anguish and perplexity" (Luke 21:25).

There would be a financial sign—the great amassing of wealth. "You have hoarded wealth in the last days" (James 5:3).

There would be a Jewish sign. In the light of the astounding Six-Day War in June 1967 between Israel and the Arab world and the liberation of Jerusalem from the kind of external domination that had prevailed until then, our Lord's prediction is most significant. "Jerusalem will be trampled on by the Gentiles until the times of the Gentiles are fulfilled" (Luke 21:24). In the same discourse He referred to the budding of the fig tree—a symbol of the quickening into national life of Israel—and said, "When you see these things happening, you know that the kingdom of God is near" (Luke 21:31).

There would be an evangelistic sign. "And this gospel of the kingdom will be preached in the whole world as a testimony to all nations, and then the end will come" (Matthew 24:14). "The gospel must first be preached to all nations" (Mark 13:10). The great missionary activity of our day has resulted in Christianity's becoming for the first time a universal religion. There does not remain any major national group in which the church of Christ has not been established.

With the fulfillment of these signs so evidently before our eyes, we have abundant warrant for believing that "[He] is near, right at the door" (Mark 13:29). (31 Days)

Life in Heaven

Matthew 8:11

Will we know one another in heaven? To many, this is the paramount question about life after death. Uncertainty as to the answer has dulled the desire of heaven for some. It would be no blissful place for them if they were unable to recognize friends and loved ones of the past. One of the anticipatory joys of heaven is the prospect of reunion. Our question has been expressed poignantly in verse by Robert Browning.

> When the holy angels meet us
> As we go to join their band,
> Shall we know the friends that greet us
> In the glorious spirit-land?

To that question J. H. Bavinck gives the following confident answer, an answer that has abundant support in Scripture: "The hope to see one another in heaven is entirely natural, genuinely human and in harmony with Scripture." Life in heaven will bring enrichment, not impoverishment. The author George MacDonald once posed the question in a humorous way, "Shall we be greater fools in Paradise than we are here?"

No Scripture passage suggests the abolition of all former relationships when we arrive in heaven. In a letter to Canon Barry, Sir William Robertson Nicoll, the noted religious editor, referring to the poet Robert Browning's views on this subject said:

> "What I gathered from Browning ... was that our personalities are distinct in the next world, and that a pure and holy love between individuals in this life is a creation of God, and will live on in the next."

It is the essential element of personality that will persist after death, not the temporary "tent" in which it is housed on this earth. The body is destined to return to dust, but the inward man, the spirit, lives on, and its identity with the body is not breached.

Angels have no bodies, and yet they exist and act as distinct personalities. If angels who have no bodies are able to recognize one another, why should this not be possible for believers? In Daniel 9:21 and 10:13 it is recorded that Michael the archangel came to the assistance of his colleague Gabriel when the latter was hindered in his mission by satanic beings. If angels, why not men and women? (HB)

Final Justice

Psalm 73:16–17

B ecause of human sin, life on earth is clearly unjust. If God is as good and just as the Scriptures state and as we have maintained, how can He retain His character while permitting such a state of affairs to continue? If He remains inactive in this situation, it would appear that He is either uncaring or is powerless to correct and judge the many injustices of this life.

But both Scripture and history are filled with declarations that He is neither uncaring nor inactive. This life is not the end of all that there is. Such inequalities will be made right.

Where did Asaph discover the solution to his problem? He tells us, "Surely in vain I have kept my heart pure and have washed my hands in innocence . . . When I tried to understand all this, it troubled me deeply till I entered the sanctuary of God; then I understood their final destiny" (Psalm 73:13, 16–17). Like him, we should take our perplexing problems into the presence of God and try to see things from His perspective. It is the end view that is important.

Scripture is filled with prophetic statements that a day is coming when injustices will be rectified and inequalities balanced out, when evil will be punished and virtue appropriately rewarded. This will take place at the day of judgment. Those who in this life have not availed themselves of the only way of salvation through the grace of God and the atoning death of Christ will not enter the gates of heaven. The Word is uncompromising: "Nothing impure will ever enter it, nor will anyone who does what is shameful or deceitful, but only those whose names are written in the Lamb's book of life" (Revelation 21:27). (HB)

Death Is Not Final

1 Corinthians 15:3

"I delivered to you as of first importance what I also received, that Christ died for our sins" (1 Corinthians 15:3 NASB). This act takes front rank in Paul's theology. All other truths derive their meaning from this great central tenet of the Christian faith. In thinking of the cross, our emphasis tends to be too much on its physical aspects—and those were incredibly terrible—but our Lord repeatedly indicated that the bodily aspect of things was only secondary. Even death is not primarily a thing of the flesh. Jesus insisted on referring to physical and visible death as "sleep," much to the mystification of His disciples.

Of Jairus's daughter, He said, "She is not dead, but sleepeth" (Luke 8:52 KJV). Of Lazarus He said, "Our friend Lazarus sleepeth" (John 11:11 KJV). But the disciples were so obtuse that Jesus had to spell it out plainly for them: "Lazarus is dead" (John 11:14 KJV). It is clear that our concept of physical death He called "sleep." Paul follows in the steps of his Master by using His same gentle metaphor: "them also which sleep in Jesus," "them which are asleep" (1 Thessalonians 4:14–15 KJV).

Christ repeatedly declared that He came to save us from death. "If a man keep my saying, he shall never see death" (John 8:51 KJV). Yet the saintliest soul is laid to rest in the same cemetery as the most godless. Our interpretation of death is obviously different from His.

But Christ did more than "sleep"! "He died for all." We see Him on Calvary, His face drawn in agony, His quivering body dripping blood. We hear His last gasp. But that physical cessation which we call death, He called sleep. Death meant something infinitely more terrible. Many of His followers were crucified, but they did not die—they only slept.

In Gethsemane Jesus had not begun to sleep, but He had begun to die. "My soul is exceeding sorrowful, even unto death" (Matthew 26:38 KJV). The deepening darkness, the dreadful cup, the desolation, the weight of the world's sin, and the averted face of His Father: this was *death*. He "taste[d] death for every man" (Hebrews 2:9 KJV). He died that we may never know the damning sting of death, but will be safe in His loving arms. Why should we fear the experience of physical death? It ends in glory for those who are Christ's. (CC)

Signs of Christ's Return

Luke 21:24

To a unique degree this generation has witnessed the universal and dramatic fulfillment of prophecy. Many of the signs Jesus said would herald His return have developed before our eyes.

The Evangelistic Sign. "This gospel of the kingdom will be preached in the whole world as a testimony to all nations, and then the end will come" (Matthew 24:14).

This prophecy has been fulfilled in our generation to a degree that has never before been the case. There is now no major nation in which there is no Christian witness. But as Christ has not yet returned, it is obvious that our task has not been fully completed.

The Religious Sign. "That day will not come until the rebellion occurs and the man of lawlessness is revealed" (2 Thessalonians 2:3).

Unfortunately, we can see this sign being fulfilled all around us. As Jesus foretold, the love of many is growing cold (Matthew 24:12). But also in many parts of the world there is an unprecedented gathering of the harvest, so we do not need to be discouraged.

The Political Sign. Could prevailing world conditions have been more accurately and comprehensively described than in our Lord's words in Luke 21:25–26? "There will be signs ... On the earth, nations will be in anguish and perplexity ... People will faint from terror, apprehensive of what is coming on the world."

The Jewish Sign. "Jerusalem will be trampled on by the Gentiles until the times of the Gentiles are fulfilled" (Luke 21:24).

There are broad and general signs that Jesus gave to His disciples as precursors of His return. These and many other signs have been intensified and have come to fulfillment in our day. For the first time in 2,500 years, Jerusalem is not dominated by Gentiles.

Whatever view we hold regarding the details surrounding the second coming of Christ, if we fail to discern in these broad signs an intimation of the imminence of His return, we should deserve a similar rebuke. History is moving rapidly—not to cataclysm merely, but to consummation. (SD)

Focus on the Eternal

Galatians 6:9

aul had just written, "We look not at the things which are
seen, but at the things which are not seen; for the things
which are seen are temporal, but the things which are not
seen are eternal" (2 Corinthians 4:18 NASB). For him death
held no terrors because he was mastered by the powers of the
world to come.

When our gaze is concentrated on the things around us—
political revolution, industrial chaos, economic instability,
war, crime, violence, lawlessness, the diminishing sanctity
of marriage—we see much to discourage us and little to kindle
optimism. But Paul exhorts us to lift our eyes and focus
on eternal values. He reminds us that the Christian is not
to walk according to the dictates of sight but by faith in the
eternal and all-powerful God.

Peter looked at his Lord and triumphantly walked on the
unstable waves. When he shifted his gaze and became
engrossed with the waves, he was engulfed. When will we
master that elementary lesson of the spiritual life?

For the Christian worker there are temptations to dis-
couragement and loss of heart over the lack of visible evidence

of success. We give ourselves to our task without reservation. We pray and work and sometimes weep, and yet the harvest tarries, and we tend to falter. Our wily adversary Satan plays his cards shrewdly at such times, and we sometimes fail to detect his strategy and fall into his snare.

The time factor in Galatians 6:9 is important—"at the proper time." There is always an interval between sowing and reaping. The process of germination and maturation takes time and is largely invisible. But "at the proper time," harvest is certain.

So let us not grow tired, and let us not lose heart, for "he who goes to and fro weeping, carrying his bag of seed, shall indeed come again with a shout of joy, bringing his sheaves with him" (Psalm 126:6 NASB). (EI)

The Slowness of God

Romans 4:19–21

In time of war, bleeding hearts cry, "God could bring all this slaughter and bloodshed to an end in a moment. Why does He wait? Why does He not intervene?"

Why not? It is certainly not because He is physically unable or that He is unwilling to do so. The only answer is that He is *morally* unable to do so. We must recognize that there are things that are moral and spiritual impossibilities to God. He cannot lie. He cannot deny himself. He cannot save a sinful person apart from repentance and faith. God does not glory in war and bloodshed, and He will intervene when it is morally right to do so. When He sees a nation bow in humiliation and confession of its national sins, it becomes possible and right for Him to intervene. When wicked Nineveh publicly expressed its repentance, God immediately responded by lifting the judgment. It is not God who is too slow, but people who are too sinful.

How slow God sometimes seems in granting the answer to our prayers! Months and even years go by and yet there is no apparent response. George Muller prayed for more than sixty years for the salvation of two men. The answer came in the case of one of the men just before Muller's death and the other one shortly after. What a long, drawn-out test of faith this was, but how wonderful the prayer of faith proved to be to the one who prayed.

Sometimes God is slow in granting the answer to our prayers so that we may learn lessons we could master in no other way. We pray for the salvation or the sanctification of our children, and the answer sometimes seems more remote than ever. But God has not forgotten His promises. It is for us to maintain the attitude of confident faith as exemplified by Abraham, who relied on the Word of God.

"Without weakening in his faith, he faced the fact. . . . Yet he did not waver through unbelief regarding the promise of God, but was strengthened in his faith . . . being fully persuaded that God had power to do what he had promised" (Romans 4:19–21). (SP)

Who Is on Trial?

John 19:11

Throughout the crowded closing hours of His life, Jesus said nothing that could in any way be construed as a withdrawal or watering down of the astounding claims to kingship and deity He had made. Although He did not disallow the claim that He was King, He hastened to make clear that His kingdom was not of this world but was a spiritual one (John 18:36). Nor did He deny that He was "the Messiah, the Son of the Blessed One" (Mark 14:61) but quietly accepted the title. In the face of such a statement, it is difficult to understand how hostile critics can suggest as they do that He never claimed deity for himself. He always spoke and acted in a manner entirely consistent with such a claim.

Nothing could be more impressive than His total indifference to the insults and threats of His unscrupulous judges. For various reasons Pilate obviously desired to release Jesus, but He did nothing to make it easy for Pilate to do so or to assist him in this goal. He was certainly an unusual prisoner in this regard.

When Pilate suggested that he would listen favorably to Him, much to the governors' amazement, Jesus did not even try to answer. He showed not the slightest interest in Pilate's repeated endeavors to secure His release, whether by dissuading the Jews from pressing their demand or by persuading them to accept Barabbas the murderer instead of Jesus the Holy One.

When for the last time Pilate sought to release Jesus, he said, "Do you refuse to speak to me? . . . Don't you realize I have power either to free you or to crucify you?" (John 19:10). Jesus answered, "You would have no power over me if it were not given to you from above" (v. 11). Both by His silence and His words, Jesus made clear that it was Pilate and the Jews who were on trial before Him, and not He before them. (31 Days)

God's Veto

Hebrews 12:10

If God should veto a certain course of action on which your heart is set, be assured that He has not done it out of caprice. It is because of His deep concern that you do not miss the best He has for you. It is the expression of His perfect wisdom and love. "God disciplines us for our good, in order that we may share in his holiness" (Hebrews 12:10). It is the best wisdom to wait for the gradual unfolding of God's will in providence.

Sometimes when our cherished plans are checkmated, it is not denial, only delay for some wise purpose. The experience of the Israelites immediately after their deliverance from Egypt is a case in point. From the place where they crossed the Red Sea to the borders of Canaan at Kadesh Barnea, the journey would normally take only eleven days (Deuteronomy 1:2). Taking the route they traveled, however, it took them several months.

It must be remembered that the Israelites had lived as slaves all their lives; others made the decisions for them. So God in His compassion allowed them sufficient time to adjust to their new status.

The wisdom of this detour soon became apparent. When they began to meet opposition and the going became difficult, they soon showed how ill prepared they were for the conflict and hardships that lay ahead. They desperately needed the brief but gentle initiation of the desert experience to toughen and mature them and fit them for conflict against war-experienced foes.

So does God at times lead His servants on what seems like a pointless detour. His leading crosses our desires and inclinations because He is working for eternity and has deeper purposes in view. (EL)

Growing in Wisdom

Luke 2:52

J esus advanced in mental capacity. "Jesus grew in wisdom"
(Luke 2:52). He was not an adult infant. He acquired the
power of speech as did other children. He gradually gained
familiarity with the ordinary branches of human knowledge.
He learned to read (Luke 4:17) and write (John 8:6–8). His
knowledge came to Him by degrees, but every degree
of growth was perfect.

So body and mind developed together, and He displayed
manly vigor and mental prowess. It is impossible to penetrate
the mystery of His gradual development, but Scripture
asserts it as a fact.

Although the Gospels shed no light on the education
of Jesus, it is possible to gain some knowledge from the cus-
toms of the day. His first instruction was at the knee of His
mother. She would teach Him to chant psalms and would
instruct Him in the basics of the Hebrew law and history.
From the preparations for the Passover festival, He would
be told the story of redemption in the Old Testament.

In a Jewish village the size of Nazareth there would be
a school, known as "The House of the Book," to which Jesus

would be sent at the age of six. The rulers of the synagogue were the teachers. Up to the age of ten, the Old Testament Scriptures were the only textbook. For five years the children memorized the Old Testament (Deuteronomy 6:7), especially the Pentateuch, until "the Jew knew the Law better than his own name." From His familiarity with the Scriptures, there was probably a copy of the sacred scrolls in the home.

The first book to be studied was Leviticus. What were the thoughts that jostled in the mind of the eager young scholar as He read the ritual of sacrifice that foreshadowed the sacrifice of God's Lamb? James Stalker remarks that no stain of sin clouded His vision of divine things, and His soul would have inklings, growing to convictions, that He was One in whom their predictions were destined to be realized. (31 Days)

Rich Yet Poor

2 Corinthians 8:9

"Ye know the grace of our Lord Jesus Christ, that, though he was rich, yet for your sakes he became poor, that ye through his poverty might be rich" (2 Corinthians 8:9 KJV). We are presented here with a striking antithesis—the unutterable poverty that is ours and the unsearchable riches that are Christ's. Our deep poverty serves as a black background to display the magnificence of His riches.

In relation to what is of supreme and eternal value, we are tragically poor. Our poverty may not be financial, but money is the lowest form of riches. The true value of life cannot be calculated in dollars and cents. Indeed, money has a subtle way of distracting us from what is most precious in life. The highest riches are not material but moral and spiritual, and our assets in this latter realm are pitifully meager.

What riches does Christ possess? He is heir of all things. He shared the glory of the Father. He was one with Him in a relationship of unbroken harmony. To be loved is one of life's richest experiences, and Christ enjoyed the infinite love and intimacy of the Father and of His holy angels. He said, "Thou lovedst me before the foundation of the world" (John 17:24 KJV), and His capacity to enjoy that love was infinite. How rich He was!

But "for [our] sakes he became poor," and how poor compared to His former stature! In His incarnation, He exchanged heaven's purple robes of royalty for a peasant robe; His Father's love for the illogical hatred of people. He relinquished heaven's harmony for earth's strife. He was denounced as a glutton, a drunkard, and a demon-possessed man. In heaven they cried, "Holy, holy." On earth it was, "Crucify, crucify!" Once He had been daily His Father's delight, now His Father's face was turned away. Once He had created unnumbered worlds; now He bowed His head and dismissed His spirit on the cross.

His poverty ensures our spiritual enrichment with the outcome of eternal life. Paul was writing to Corinthian Christians who were far from perfect when he said, "that [you] through his poverty might be rich." It would have been wonderful to receive a few crumbs from His table, but He makes us joint heirs with himself. What wonderful grace from our wonderful Lord! (CC)

The Humble Carpenter

Hebrews 2:17

It is not difficult to conceive the wonder and perplexity of the angelic host who saw the great Jehovah, Creator of the rolling spheres, humble himself to toil with saw and hammer at a carpenter's bench for eighteen years. They would see Him who made the heavens stoop to shape with His own hands a yoke for oxen.

Whatever else this act of humility signified, it meant that Jesus identified himself fully with the great bulk of humanity, the common people. It gave common people's toil everlasting honor. It acquainted the Master with the feelings of these common people and gave Him insight into their inmost thoughts. His willingness to occupy so lowly a sphere for so long a time gives us both an example and incentive to be willing to do our common tasks joyously.

In common with all other Jewish boys, Jesus was required to learn a trade. What was more natural than that He should be apprenticed to His foster father and become the village carpenter? In this connection remember that in keeping with the custom of the times, Paul mastered the intricacies of the tentmaker's art as well as his university studies.

It is a challenging thought, and one that should be closely observed by those who are preparing for a life of service for God, that our divine Lord spent six times as long working at the carpenter's bench as He did in His world-shaking ministry. He did not cut short the hidden years of preparation. Jesus must be about His Father's business and doing His Father's will. If that will involved eighteen hidden, laborious, and tedious years, He would not give in to fleshly impatience but would obey with delight. "I desire to do your will, my God; your law is within my heart" (Psalm 40:8). It should be remembered that in those times the trade of a carpenter was not considered dishonorable. It was a vocation from which it was still possible to become a rabbi.

The meekness exhibited by Jesus in working as a carpenter is all the more remarkable in the light of His subsequent amazing miracles. He could have dazzled the world with the display of His supernatural power. Instead, He worked as hard as any other man in order that in all things He might be "made like [his brothers]" (Hebrews 2:17). (31 Days)

Moral Perfection

Isaiah 53:2

In a letter published after his death, the poet Robert Browning cited several statements of men of learning concerning the Christian faith, and among them was this one from Charles Lamb: "In trying to predict with some friends as to how they would react if some of the great persons of past ages were to appear suddenly in the flesh once more, one of the friends said, 'And if Christ entered this room?' Lamb changed his attitude at once and said, 'You see if Shakespeare entered we should all rise; if He appeared, we must kneel.'" This was his view of the glory of Christ.

A brilliant Hindu scholar drew a similar conclusion. Disturbed by the progress of the Christian faith among his own people, he determined to do all in his power to arrest it. His plan was to prepare a book for widespread distribution highlighting the weaknesses and failings of Christ and exposing the fallacy of believing in Him.

For eleven years he diligently studied the New Testament, searching for inconsistencies in Christ's character and teaching. Not only did he fail to discover any, but he became convinced that the One he sought to discredit was who

He claimed to be—the Son of God. The scholar then boldly confessed his faith in Christ.

The moral perfection of Christ impresses itself on the serious reader of the Gospels. The evangelists present the portrait of a real man who displays perfection at every stage of His development and in every circumstance of His life. This is all the more remarkable as He did not lock himself in some secluded cloister but mixed freely and naturally with the imperfect people of His own generation. He became so deeply involved in the life of the ordinary people that His tendency to mix with sinners drew the most bitter criticism of the sanctimonious Pharisees.

And yet He seemed so ordinary that many of His contemporaries saw Him only as "the carpenter's son," a lowly Nazarene. With eyes blinded by sin and selfishness, they saw no beauty in Him that they should desire Him (Isaiah 53:2). To all except those whose eyes were enlightened by love and faith, His moral grandeur and divine glory passed unnoticed. (31 Days)

The Breath of God

Ezekiel 37:9

I t was the breath of God that produced order out of chaos in the beginning (Genesis 1:2). Man became a living soul by God's breathing into his nostrils the breath of life (Genesis 2:7). Ezekiel witnessed lifeless corpses become a living army when in obedience to the divine command he prayed, "Come from the four winds, O breath, and breathe upon these slain, that they may live" (37:9 KJV).

With this in mind, let us consider the symbolic act of Christ, in which He graphically revealed to His disciples the source of their power. First, there was the twice-repeated blessing of peace (John 20:19, 21). Next, the Great Commission: "As my Father hath sent me, even so send I you" (20:21 KJV). Then the imparting of the Spirit: "He breathed on [into] them, and saith unto them, Receive ye the Holy Ghost" (v. 22 KJV), without whose aid they would be powerless to execute His commission. This was a miniature anticipation of the full-scale outpouring of the Spirit at Pentecost and teaches us a valuable lesson. It was as though He were saying, "All you have to do is to breathe in, to take the Holy Spirit I impart to you now. He is the power who enables you to fulfill my commission."

This graphic expiration and inspiration is the way the Spirit is received. The disciples breathed in what Christ breathed out. Could any illustration be as simple? On the Day of Pentecost God breathed out, and there came from heaven a sound like a rushing mighty wind, meaning breath. They breathed in, and they were all filled with the Holy Ghost. Breathing in is simply the equivalent of receiving. When we breathe in, the same life-giving qualities as are in the atmosphere come into us. When we breathe in or receive the Holy Spirit, that which is peculiar to Him becomes peculiar to us, just as when we place iron in the fire, the fire enters the iron and the iron partakes of the properties peculiar to the fire. (SM)

He Is Worthy

1 Timothy 3:16

We are by nature essentially selfish beings. And even after we have been made partakers of the divine nature, so strong is the power of the old life that we are usually more interested in receiving than in giving. Was not our Lord's statement "It is more blessed to give than to receive" (Acts 20:35) a tacit correction of this tendency? In our relationship with God we are constantly at the receiving end. We commence our Christian life by receiving the atonement (Romans 5:11). We continue our Christian life by receiving the abundance of grace (Romans 5:17). We conclude our Christian life by being received into glory (1 Timothy 3:16). We are constantly tugging at God's skirts for some desired blessing, and He delights to have it so, but we forget that He too yearns to receive from us what we alone can give Him.

In one sense we cannot enrich Christ. But nothing is more heartening to Him than the spontaneous voicing of our appreciation of His intrinsic worth, and nothing is more enriching to ourselves, for it is in the process of being worshiped that God communicates His presence to people.

Writing in this connection, C. S. Lewis says,

To see what the doctrine really means, we must suppose ourselves to be in perfect love with God—drunk with, drowned in, dissolved by that delight which, far from remaining pent up within ourselves as incommunicable, hence hardly tolerable bliss, flows out from us incessantly again in effortless and perfect expression, our joy no more separable from the praise in which it liberates and utters itself than the brightness of a mirror is separable from the brightness it sheds. The Scottish catechism says that man's chief end is "to glorify God and to enjoy Him forever." But we shall then know that these are the same thing. Fully to enjoy is to glorify. In commanding us to glorify Him, God is inviting us to enjoy Him. (SM)

He Is without Sin

John 17:4

The Lord's challenge to His critics still remains unanswered: "Can any of you prove me guilty of sin?" (John 8:46). His sinlessness could not be challenged, or they would have brought a charge against Him. Even hell could bring no accusation. "The prince of this world is coming. He has no hold over me," Jesus claimed (John 14:30).

A study of His life reveals consistent immunity from sin. Never did He show the slightest discontent with His own behavior—which would be a grave sin of pride in any other person. Never did He shed a tear over any failure. He demanded repentance of others yet was never penitent himself. Nor can this self-satisfaction be explained on the grounds that His standard of duty or sense of moral obligation was less exacting than that of His contemporaries. The reverse was the case. His code of ethics was immeasurably higher than theirs, yet not once does He admit that He has in any degree fallen short of His own exacting standards.

At the end of His life, as Jesus communed with His Father in His moving High Priestly Prayer, He claimed to have accomplished perfectly the work entrusted to Him

(John 17:4). In any other case than His, we would be justified in regarding such claims as obnoxious pride and arrogant hypocrisy. In His case the facts substantiated the claim.

To quote T. C. Edwards in this context, "The fact that Jesus never confessed sin implies in His case that He never did sin. In every other good man, the saintlier he becomes the more pitiless is his self-condemnation, and the more severe he is on certain kinds of sin, such as hypocrisy. But Jesus, if He were a sinner, was guilty of the very worst of sin, which He rebuked with burning anger in the Pharisees of His day. Yet He never accuses himself . . . He never speaks about redeeming himself but declares himself to be the paschal lamb 'whose blood of the new covenant is shed for many unto the remission of sins'" (see Matthew 26:28).

While describing the doom of the unrepentant in terrible images, He never mentions His own need for salvation. He prayed, "Father, forgive them," but never, "Father, forgive Me." (31 Days)

Christ's Victory over Satan

Romans 8:33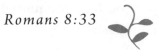

Jesus triumphed over Satan in the wilderness and "returned ... in the power of the Spirit" (Luke 4:1–14). By His death on Calvary, He bound "a strong man fully armed" and took away from him "his armor on which he had relied, and distributes his plunder" (Luke 11:21–22 NASB).

By His vicarious death and victorious resurrection, Christ once and for all answered every charge or accusation that Satan could bring against the child of God. This truth caused Paul to ask his triumphant questions: "Who will bring a charge against God's elect? ... Who is the one who condemns?" (Romans 8:33–34 NASB). This truth inspired John's ringing declaration: "Now the salvation, and the power, and the kingdom of our God and the authority of His Christ have come, for the accuser of our brethren has been thrown down, who accuses them before our God day and night" (Revelation 12:10 NASB).

Paul further expounds Christ's victory over Satan through the illustration of the exultant march of a victorious Roman general returning after a triumphant campaign. His reward was to march his army through the streets of Rome, leading behind him the captive, weaponless kings and peoples he had conquered. He boldly displayed them as his conquests.

This is the picture in Colossians 2:15. God made a public example and exposed to public disgrace the evil principalities and powers, showing to all that the victory of Calvary had disarmed them and left them impotent. Satan and his hosts have only as much power over the believer as he allows them to have. For did not Christ say, "I have given you authority ... to overcome *all* the power of the enemy" (Luke 10:19, emphasis added)? Their power over humanity is forever broken. Christ's victory over Satan is our victory over Satan, and it is complete. (SM)

The Lordship of Christ

Romans 14:9

The lordship of Christ was a constant emphasis of the apostle Paul. As he used the term in his writings, the title *Lord* uniformly denoted Christ. In his initial surrender, Paul embraced without reservation Christ's lordship and absolute mastery over his life. This totality of commitment was implicit in his question, "What shall I do, Lord?" (Acts 22:10). With quick spiritual insight, he realized that the purpose of Christ's death and resurrection went far beyond the mere salvation of the believer from judgment, but confirmed the authenticity of his lordship.

Paul later expressed the importance of Christ's lordship in these words: "For this very reason, Christ died and returned to life so that he might be the Lord of both the dead and the living" (Romans 14:9). It was the apostle's constant joy to emphasize "the crown rights of the Redeemer."

The greatest Christological passage in the New Testament comes from Paul's pen in Philippians 2:5–11. In this poetic confession of faith, he first affirms the humiliation of the Son of God, calling attention to the Son's preexistence, incarnation, and crucifixion. Paul then unfolds the exaltation of the Son of Man, who shall be honored and worshiped eventually by all creation. In view of these glorious truths, the apostle exhorts, "Let this mind be in you, which was also in Christ Jesus" (Philippians 2:5 KJV).

"In Christ" is a particular phrase that appears quite often in many contexts in Paul's writings, a phrase that is especially pregnant with meaning. The idea behind the phrase seems to be that just as the sea is the sphere or element in which fish live, so Christians live in the sphere or element of Christ, joined to Him by an invisible yet inseparable bond. Every spiritual blessing is ours because we are *in Christ*—in a living, vital union with Him (Ephesians 1:3). (PL)

Ascension into Heaven

John 3:13

The ascension was a divine vindication of Jesus's claims to deity that had been rejected by the Jews. He had claimed the right to ascend into heaven as His own prerogative. "No one has ever gone into heaven except the one who came from heaven—the Son of Man" (John 3:13).

Finally, it was time for His divine inauguration into His heavenly priesthood, sitting at the right hand of God. For the believer, our Lord's ascension has blessed implications for us. Though physically remote, He is always spiritually near. Now that He is free from earthly limitations, His life above is both the promise and the guarantee of our life to come. "Because I live, you also will live," He assured His disciples (John 14:19). His ascension anticipates our glorification and leaves us the assurance that He has gone to prepare a place for us (John 14:2).

His resurrection and ascension to heaven involved nothing less than making His humanity eternal in a transfigured and glorified form, even if it may be wholly incomprehensible to us at present. It still brings Him very near to us as we remember that He carried His humanity back with Him to heaven (Hebrews 2:14–18).

"He led captivity captive" (Ephesians 4:8 KJV). His ascension was His triumphant return to heaven and indicated that the tyrannical reign of sin was ended and His reign was underway.

R. H. Laver writes:

> The ascension helped to clarify the nature of the role of the Messiah to the apostles. They expected a Davidic king, whereas the crucifixion presented them with a suffering Servant. Then the resurrection proclaimed a king after all. The ascension further clarified the nature of His Kingship. The Kingdom of Christ is indeed not of this world. He will reign, but it shall not be simply from an earthly throne. His Kingdom will be glorious but it shall not be achieved through the blood and steel of men. The Cross was the decisive and atoning conflict; the resurrection was the proclamation of triumph; the ascension was the Conqueror's return with the captives of war which issued in the enthronement of the victorious King. (31 Days)

Human in Every Sense

John 11:35

Our Lord's consenting to be subject to human limitations was part of the mystery of His great self-humiliation. While in His incarnate state He did not renounce His divine powers, His knowledge was so subject to human limitations that He submitted to the ordinary laws of human development. He was no exception to the rest of humanity. He acquired His knowledge through the ordinary channels open to the other boys of His day: through instruction, study, and reflection. It would appear that He even voluntarily renounced knowledge of certain future events. "About that day or hour no one knows, not even the angels in heaven, nor the Son, but only the Father" (Mark 13:32).

Like us, Jesus was not self-sustained but needed prayer and communion with His Father for the support of His spiritual life. In all the great crises of His life, He resorted not to the counsel of men but to prayer to His Father for guidance (e.g., Luke 5:16; 6:12; 9:18, 28). He was subject to human limitations of power. He obtained the power for His divine works not by drawing on His inherent deity but by depending on the anointing Spirit (Acts 10:38).

One of the strongest evidences of the reality of His humanity was His experience of human suffering. He knew the salty taste of pain. Every nerve of His body was racked with anguish. Though He was God's Son, He was not exempt from suffering (Hebrews 5:8). His sufferings of body and of spirit have formed the theme of many books. The fact that He was sinless made Him more sensitive to pain than His sinful contemporaries, for the latter deserved pain as a consequence of sin. We read of His being in agony. The events of His death on the cross assure us of His ability to sympathize with human suffering.

He displayed the ultimate in human perfections. Both friend and foe acknowledge Him as the only perfect man. All attempts to depict a perfect character in human history, other than those of the four evangelists concerning Jesus, have failed. To conceive and portray a perfect character by an imperfect author is beyond the power of fallible, sinful man.

Then how could these Galilean fishermen create such a life? The simple answer is that they did not. They merely faithfully recorded the life of One who had lived in their midst. His inner life had been open to their scrutiny as they were in daily contact with Him.

If any fact stands out crystal clear in the New Testament, it is the complete and genuine humanity of Jesus Christ. (31 Days)

God behind the Scenes

Esther 3:5

One notable feature of the book of Esther is the absence of any mention of the name of God. But although His name is not pronounced, it is latent; and His hidden activity is everywhere to be seen by the discerning eye. In a theater, the scene-shifter is not seen, but the whole audience enjoys the benefits of that hidden activity. God does not always work ostentatiously, but He is nonetheless active, and the outcome of events will demonstrate His providential control.

Follow the timeline in the story. It seemed as though God had delayed His intervention too long, for Mordecai was to be hanged the very next morning, and no possible plan for his deliverance was apparent. Who could intervene on his behalf? But while God may not be early, He is never late. At the last possible moment, He intervened in a most natural way. When the hour struck on God's clock, the righteous man was delivered and the wicked man punished. The whole reversal of events occurred overnight and was orchestrated through a king's insomnia.

What outcome could be more fitting than the exact reversal of the positions of the wicked Haman and the virtuous

Mordecai? The honor that the former planned for himself was enjoyed by the latter, while the gallows erected for the latter were occupied by the former. Where, as seems so often the case, just retribution does not fall on the wrongdoer during this life, the certainty of final and just judgment must take place.

Whether in individual or in national affairs, all is foreseen, foreordained, and permitted. Everything proceeds under God's direction. *God's perfect plan will become plain if we have the patience to wait.* Mordecai was doubtless mystified by the apparent inactivity of God; but after his patience had been tested to the limit, it was rewarded. So even though we may not see God's fully matured plan in this life, we shall wonder as we see it unfold in the hereafter and be awed by its perfection. (SP)

The Indwelling of Christ

2 Corinthians 13:5

C hristianity is the only religion in which the founder claims to live in the very beings of those who place their faith in Him. Neither Buddha nor Muhammad made any such claim. This is the unique characteristic of the Christian faith and what makes its benefits far superior to those of other religions.

Early in His ministry, our Lord spoke about His dwelling in His followers. "At that day ye shall know that I am in my Father, and ye in me, and I in you" (John 14:20 KJV). The lover of our souls will not be content with mere influence in our lives. He must dwell in our hearts, in very intimate fellowship with us. Paul included this concept as an article of his message—"Christ in you, the hope of glory" (Colossians 1:27 KJV). John rejoiced in its reality—"Greater is he that is in you, than he that is in the world" (1 John 4:4 KJV).

This personal indwelling of Christ is both a fact to comprehend and an experience to realize. There is a difference between a fact and an experience of that fact. Whether we are conscious of it or not, Christ indwells every Christian all the time. It may seem mysterious, but so are many other things about the universe we cannot understand. I am not conscious of the blood flowing in my veins, but that does not alter the fact that it does. Through failing to realize that Christ really indwells them, many believers never go on to fully appreciate and utilize this blessed fact.

Jesus had promised, "At that day ye shall know that I am . . . in you." To what day did He refer? The answer was given on the day of Pentecost when the Holy Spirit was given as Christ's representative on earth. With the gift of the Spirit, there came to the waiting disciples an overwhelming consciousness of the spiritual presence and indwelling of the physically absent Christ that transformed them into His fearless and selfless servants.

"When it pleased God . . . to reveal His Son in [Paul]," the experience was so real and vivid to the apostle that he testified, "I am crucified with Christ: nevertheless, I live; yet not I, but Christ liveth in me" (Galatians 2:20 KJV). Do you realize that Jesus Christ is in you? (CC)

The Sacrifice of Christ

Hebrews 13:12

L ike the chosen victim, Christ was without spot or blemish. Through the miracle of the virgin birth and the activity of the Holy Spirit, He escaped the taint of original sin. His purity was essential and inherent. No matter how severe the criticism to which He was subjected during His life on earth, it was demonstrated that "in him is no sin" (1 John 3:5). The yoke of sin never rested on His shoulders, nor was it under a yoke of constraint that He consented to become the sacrifice for our sins. His sacrifice was absolutely voluntary.

Then, too, like the victim, Christ, in order "that he might sanctify the people with his own blood, suffered without the gate" of Jerusalem (Hebrews 13:12 KJV), the defiled place frequented by the lepers. The defilement was viewed as transferred to the victim that must now take the place of the defiled person—outside the camp. In this act of matchless condescension on the part of the Lord of glory, the boundless and forgiving love of God is exhibited. The sprinkling of the blood before the tabernacle did not in itself affect the cleansing of the polluted person, but before there can be purification there must first be atonement.

The burning of the cedar and hyssop bound with scarlet wool signifies that the sinful self-life, the "old man," whether in attractive or repulsive guise, was cast into the burning or, to use the New Testament terminology, was crucified with Christ, and in Him was "done away with" (Romans 6:6). The self-life will always defile and pollute us unless we put it to death (Romans 6:11). We must resolutely disregard its plea to be allowed to come down from the cross.

The ashes, evidence of a completed sacrifice, were regarded as the concentration of the essential properties of the offering. They were incorruptible, and therefore a suitable emblem of the perfection and everlasting efficacy of the sacrifice of Christ. The ashes laid up in a clean place represent the store of merit there is in the Lord Jesus, perpetually preserved for the removal of the daily pollution of sin. The smallest quantity of the concentrated ash would suffice to cleanse. Jewish tradition records that only six heifers were required in all Jewish history. "If . . . the ashes of a heifer . . . how much more will the blood of Christ . . . cleanse" (Hebrews 9:13–14 NASB)? (SP)

Heaven's Many Mansions

John 14:2–3

The Christian concept of heaven far outstrips Jewish thought. It is immeasurably higher and more detailed than Old Testament speculations. As Alexander Maclaren put it, heaven is a place of indescribable splendor, of blessedness and peace. We are left by its biblical description with an image of a life that will far transcend anything we have known so far. So incredibly glorious is it, that we are compelled to express it in both negative terms and by symbols of grandeur and majesty, "gathered," as Maclaren said, "from what is noblest and best in human building and society."

But what makes heaven what it is for the Christian is the perpetual presence of God as sovereign ruler of the universe and yet at the same time as our loving heavenly Father, and the reality of enjoying forever the companionship of our Redeemer and Lord. "God's dwelling place is now among the people, and he will dwell with them. They will be his people, and God himself will be with them and be their God" (Revelation 21:3).

Will mansions be awaiting us? "In my Father's house are many mansions: if it were not so, I would have told you.

I go to prepare a place for you. And if I go and prepare a place for you, I will come again, and receive you unto myself; that where I am, there ye may be also" (John 14:2–3 KJV).

These treasured words have imparted more comfort to dying saints and grieving relatives than any other portion of Scripture. Scottish writer Ian Maclaren [not to be confused with Alexander above] gave this testimony: "Whenever I am called to a house of sickness or sorrow, I always read to the troubled folk John 14. Nothing else is so effective. If a man is sinking into unconsciousness, and you read about many mansions, he will come back and whisper 'mansions,' and will wait until you finish—'that where I am, there you may be also.'" Ian Maclaren lived in a day when people were familiar enough with the Scriptures to finish the sentence, but today not all would recognize the allusion.

"Trust me!" our Lord urged His followers. He spoke these words on the night before the cross to His dearly loved disciples, who were devastated at the thought of His leaving them. So He encouraged them to keep on trusting Him. (HL)

The Living One

Revelation 1:18

" I am he that liveth, and was dead" (Revelation 1:18 KJV),
expressing the vivid contrast between the eternal life
inherent in Christ and His voluntary surrender to the powers
of death. Because He tasted death, He is able to say
to death-ridden humanity, "There is no need to fear death.
I have trodden that way, exhausted its power, and extracted
its sting."

"I am alive for evermore" (v. 18 KJV), for all the ages.
Death could not keep its prey. He now lives in "the power
of an endless life" (Hebrews 7:16 KJV). Others, like Lazarus,
had returned to life only to die again. Christ rose from the
dead and is alive forevermore. His having passed through
death as a man and now living in fullness of life is the basis for
our confidence, since through Him death is but the gateway
to fuller life. To a church facing the possibility of martyrdom,
this truth was urgently needed to quell their fear. The church
could not live if Christ were dead, but because Christ lives,
the church cannot die.

In saying, "[I] have the keys of hell and of death" (v. 18 KJV),
Christ wrested death in His resurrection from "him that

hath the power of death, that is the devil" (Hebrews 2:14 KJV). Hades is portrayed in Matthew 16:18 as a prison house or walled city. It is the unseen world to which death is the portal. Keys are the symbol of authority. The keys of the unseen world are in Christ's hand and with them the destiny of all people. We need have no fear of going to any place when the keys are in His nail-pierced hand. No longer need we fear the figure of the grim reaper, the king of terrors. Christ alone admits us to death and opens the way out on the other side. No one can wrest the keys from His control. Because He rose, we shall rise also.

Because this living, majestic, powerful Christ stands in the midst of His churches and holds their destiny in these hands, there is no cause for them or for us to fear. (SM)

Abbreviations

For those readers who wish to delve more deeply into the writings of J. Oswald Sanders, we have provided an abbreviation of the title of the source from which each selection was taken. The following is a list of those abbreviations and their corresponding titles. In some cases, the book has been released under more than one title.

31 Days...*31 Days on the Life of Christ*; also, *The Incomparable Christ*

BB ....*The Best That I Can Be*

BF ....*Bible Men of Faith*; also *Robust in Faith*

CC ....*Cameos of Comfort*

DA........*Divine Art of Soul Winning*

EI ....*Enjoying Intimacy with God*

EL ....*Every Life Is a Plan of God*

HB ....*Heaven: Better by Far*

HL ....*How Lost Are the Heathen*

JL ....*Just Like Us*; also *People Just Like Us*

PL ....*Paul the Leader*; also *Dynamic Spiritual Leadership*

PP.........*Praying Power Unlimited*; also *The Power of Transforming Prayer*

SC ....*A Spiritual Clinic*; also *Problems of Christian Discipleship*

SD.........*Spiritual Discipleship*; also *Shoe Leather Commitment, The Joy of Following Jesus*

SM ....*Spiritual Maturity*; also *On to Maturity*

SN.........*Satan Is No Myth*

SP..........*Spiritual Problems*; also *Spiritual Lessons*

About the Author

J. Oswald Sanders was the third child of Alfred and Margaret Sanders, immigrants to New Zealand from the United Kingdom. He studied law, which he practiced briefly, but his life was profoundly impacted in 1921 when he responded to an invitation to dedicate his life to serve on the mission field.

J. O., as he was known, began in an administrative post with the China Inland Mission and eventually held key positions in the Bible College of New Zealand and other Christian organizations. He also became the editor of *The Reaper*, the country's largest interdenominational magazine. Yet he was much better known as a writer of books. His passion was to train people who were called to serve Christ full-time on the mission field. His first book on evangelism, *The Divine Art of Soul Winning,* was published in 1937. It was the first of more than forty titles he would publish during his lifetime. His final book, Enjoying Your Best Years, focused on ways we can serve the Lord more fully in our later years—a lesson he modeled by his continuing service.

In 1954 he became the fifth general director of the China Inland Mission, now OMF International. Upon his retirement as OMF General Director in 1969, Dr. Sanders served as principal of the Christian Leaders Training College in Papua New Guinea. In 1980 he was given an Order of the British Empire award in honor of his work with the New Zealand Bible College, and in 1992 he was conferred an honorary doctorate in theology on the seventieth anniversary of the college.

Enjoy this book? Help us get the word out!

Share a link to the book or
mention it on social media

Write a review on your blog, on a retailer site,
or on our website (dhp.org)

Pick up another copy to share with someone

Recommend this book for your
church, book club, or small group

Follow Discovery House on
social media and join the discussion

Contact us to share your thoughts:

 @discoveryhouse    @DiscoveryHouse

Discovery House
P.O. Box 3566
Grand Rapids, MI 49501 USA

Phone: 1-800-653-8333
Email: books@dhp.org
Web: dhp.org